A Little Light from Luke

First Edition

By Felix Dailey

June 2015

Title: A Little Light from Luke

Author: Felix Dailey

Published by: Engedi Publishing LLC

First Edition, June 2015

Published in the United States of America

FOREWORD

The Bible, the Word of God, the Scriptures are some of the most common references to God's publication which contains His plan and purpose for each and every life. I trusted Jesus Christ as my Savior and committed my life to Him in 1954, and immediately He gave me an insatiable desire to discover what He had for me in His Word.

The Bible became alive, and it seemed that everything in it was relevant and applicable to my life. The scriptures seemed to speak to me about my personal life, about my relationships at work, and about my responsibility to share and live out these teachings with my family to the best of my ability.

There came a deep burden on me to somehow see to it that my children got involved in the Word. I began to realize that unless they learned to experience those unspeakable riches for themselves, they would become dull and ineffective in their relationship with the Lord. My prayers became directed toward asking God to help them have this same desire for His Word and to show them that all the answers to life's questions are contained in these inspired Scriptures.

It was then that I decided to write a book just for my children. This book was to contain four pages. On the first page would be these words "Learn the Word." On the following pages would be, "Teach it to Your Children," "Teach it to Them Better than I Taught It to You," and finally, "Teach Them to Learn it on Their Own." Like any good husband, I shared this with my wife, Frances, and assigned her the task of preparing this book.

Time went by and over the years she became caught up in the Word just as I had. She became involved in Bible Study Fellowship which was the greatest force in her life toward dedicated Bible study. She became insistent that I prepare devotional material for our family. At this time Linda and David, our two older children, were married and starting families of their own, but Michael our youngest, was still at home. I resisted, but Frances was convinced that the head of the home, the spiritual leader of the home, should read the Bible and prepare a word to share with the family at the beginning of each day.

I started prayerfully reading the book of Luke and writing what seemed to come from God as a word for my family and me. My mind went back to that time I determined to write a book for my children, and a new excitement rose up in my heart. I could imagine my children reading these simple words that were written as God gave me direction. I could see my grandchildren and my great-grandchildren reading this book after I was gone.

I began to share these writings with Frances and Michael who encouraged me to publish this. Here it is. I dedicate it to my beloved wife, Frances, and to my wonderful children, Linda, David, and Michael. I hope and pray it will send you to the Word, to learn it on your own, to learn it better than I did, to teach it to your family, and to teach your family to learn it on their own.

I would like to give a special word of thanks to Bill and Anita Hopkins who encouraged me with their love and patience and proof-reading the original text of this book.

My friend and brother in Christ, Andy Spencer carried me through the process of publishing this book. Without his encouragement and guidance, it would not have happened. Thanks Andy!

Chapter 1

Felix Dailey

First, please understand that I am not a preacher or a formally educated theologian. As the youngest of eight children, I was born and raised on a large farm in east Texas. My mother died one month before my tenth birthday, and my father died when I was a junior in high school in the small town of Grapeland, Texas. During my high school and college years, at one time or another, I lived with my sister and three of my older brothers along with their families. Living in these situations of varying rules and personalities, I was motivated to develop a strong drive of independence. Eventually I developed a drive to be completely self-sufficient. I felt I could handle any situation and accomplish any goal I desired.

I graduated from Texas A&M University in 1950 with a B.S. in petroleum engineering. My brother, Dan, who is four years older than me, graduated from A&M the same day with the same degree. He started college late due to service in Europe during World War II. Our older brothers and sister kept our dad's estate together after his death, until Dan and I were able to complete college. This was a very unselfish act on their part that impacts me to this day. Although the estate was modest, it was money they could have used, and yet they chose to wait.

By this time, my self-sufficient attitude was well in place. After graduating, Dan and I tried to get positions as engineers at various companies, but the job market was flooded at the time. As a result, I started work as a "roughneck" on a drilling rig in south Texas, and Dan went with Gulf oil as "roustabout." After six months, the company moved me into their office in Alice, Texas, as Assistant to the Drilling Superintendent, George Standard, who was part owner of the company. This man was one of the kindest, most unselfish men I have ever known. He patiently taught me more about drilling and operating oil and gas wells than any other person in my career.

Things were going great for me. I was assuming more and more responsibility and challenging opportunities at work. In March 1951, I married Joy Ann Hoherd, the young lady I dated during my final year at A&M. She was a member of the "Aggie-etts," a group of women attending Temple Junior College. The Aggie-etts organized after some men at Temple Junior College black balled them for dating Aggies. They formed the Aggie-etts in order to date Aggies exclusively. Naturally, news of this club spread quickly among the young men of Aggieland, and we acted promptly.

It was 1951, I was married and had a good job. Things were looking rosy, and that's when Uncle Sam called me up to serve in the army during the Korean war. In those days, men who were in the Corps of Cadets that graduated from A&M would automatically receive a commission as a second Lieutenant (or Ensign) in the reserves of the armed services. So we moved to Temple, Texas, to live with Joy's parents while I trained at Fort Hood in preparation for active combat duty as a second lieutenant. Once completed, we moved to Columbus, Georgia, where I underwent combat officer training at Fort Benning. The school motto is "follow me" and this embodies the mind-set for all attendees.

After I completed this training in the spring of 1952, Joy moved back to her parent's home and I was on my way to my deployment in Korea. I was assigned to Easy Company, 35th regiment, 25th division of the army. We were to replace a unit on Heartbreak Ridge, and made detailed secret preparations for the operation. We completed the replacement at night and felt good about the move until daybreak, when we heard Chinese loudspeakers welcoming us to Heartbreak Ridge by specific and accurate identification of our unit.

Our regiment spent seventy-eight days on Heartbreak Ridge. I served as the leader of an 81mm mortar platoon for a time, and then as infantry platoon leader. We had bunkers and fortified trenches along the ridge, and the line was stable. We periodically experienced Chinese and North Korean infantry probes into our position and regular artillery fire. As officers, we were required to lead patrols so I had to take one out about every five to seven days. Our patrols were about ten to twelve men in size. We would go out at dark, stay all night, and return to our position on the line just before day break. Compared to what many others had to endure along this ridge earlier on in the war, I was very fortunate.

The most important thing that happened to me on Heartbreak Ridge was on a Sunday morning. Sergeant Bass, my platoon sergeant, told me the chaplain was coming for a service and asked if I would like to attend. Feeling like it would be a good show for the men to see me go tip my hat to God, I agreed to attend. I cannot remember a word the chaplain said until enemy artillery began to hit near us, to which he announced "gentlemen, I do not think God would be offended if we put our helmets back on." As I put my helmet back on, a sickening feeling came over me regarding my self-sufficiency. I realized that there were many things my self-sufficiency could not handle. At the top of the list was a relationship with God and life after death. I thought back to the faith of my parents, siblings and other relatives who lived their lives with a dependence on God. I resolved to revisit my position with God when and if I got back home.

We completed our tour of duty on Heartbreak Ridge, and our unit took up a position in reserve. Our unit was assigned to support a South Korean unit guarding prisoners of war on Koje-Do Island. We later moved back into a combat position at an outpost in the Chorwon Valley. We were a company-sized unit holding a fortified position about halfway between U.S. and enemy lines. I served out the remainder of my time in Korea at this outpost.

When I was deployed to Korea, the army flew me from San Francisco via Honolulu, Wake Island and Tokyo. When my tour was completed, they sent me home on a liberty ship. This is what most folks would refer to as a slow boat, but I didn't mind because I was on my way home. My wife met me at Fort Smith, Arkansas, where I was discharged, and we drove back to Temple from there.

We settled back in Alice, and I was able to return to my old job. We were now expecting our first child, and my experience at that Sunday morning service on Heartbreak Ridge kept coming up in my mind. We were committed to not being hypocrites in raising our children. We were going to live by our convictions, and I was uneasy with my convictions as they related to God.

One day, the pastor of First Baptist church Alice called on us, and we visited the church. The pastor made a statement that changed my life forever. I had seen men die and heard of some who burned themselves to death for some religions beliefs. Jesus's death on the cross, as painful and agonizing as it was, did not overly impress me as a "saving" experience. This pastor said "Jesus Christ tasted hell for you" and God seemed to open my heart to a new understanding of the cost of my sins. This had gone far beyond the physical pain as Jesus cried out, "My God, my God, why have you forsaken me." I received Jesus as my savior at that time and committed my life to Him as the Lord of my life. I was already a church member and had been baptized, but now I was saved, redeemed, born again and all that expressed my new personal relationship with Jesus. I later became convicted (encouraged by Christ in me) of the need to get my baptism in proper order, so I was baptized again to publicly demonstrate what Christ had done for me. Things have never been the same since that day. God gave me an insatiable appetite for His Word. Although at times it was difficult to understand, I could not get enough of it. I learned to pray for His help in understanding and living the Word. I still pray for help, realizing the best one to ask for help is the One who wrote it. We became active in a young married Bible class under the love and mentoring of Mr. and Mrs. Gay and their daughter Oleen.

Our first child, was born on July 22, 1954, and we named her Linda Beth Dailey. Everything went well with the birth, but Joy had a blood clot that lodged in her kidney. We moved her to Spohn Hospital in Corpus Christi, Texas. As a specialists worked to get the clot dissolved, things were looking good, and we were preparing to go home the next day. Later that night, a blood clot moved to her heart, and she died within a few hours. I was devastated. She had been so anxious to see Linda again. Our families were both in shock as we worked our way through the funeral services and burial.

It seems that the brightest light of His fellowship comes in the darkest days of human experience. The fondest caress of His Spirit comes during the brutal blows of life in this broken world. This was the moment I realized how inadequate my self-sufficiency would have been, had I still been depending on it. God was watching over me in my suffering, and I can tell you with certainty that He never left me or failed to guide me through this event and all the related things that followed.

Joy's sister kept Linda as I prayed to know the next step in God's path for our future. The love and help I received from our church, company associates and family were a part of God's provision. I worked on for several months and moved in with Roy & Eva May Biggs. Roy was a tool pusher working on one of our company drilling rigs. They were dear friends that God used to help me through this time.

My job was near perfect with a small close-knit group. Everyone in the company liked me and were pleased with my work. After much prayer, I felt God leading me to make a change that put Linda first, before the job that I loved so much. So I resigned my position, took Linda and moved back to Grapeland, Texas. Once again I went to live with my brother Mike, and his wife, Hazel. They had two children at this time, Joyce Ann and Jimmy. Mike and I farmed together, and we were a big happy family. Mike and I worked daylight to dark, while Hazel and Linda bonded.

After a year of farming, I had the opportunity to go back to the "oil patch." Hazel knew a widowed mother of two named Bernice who agreed to move to San Antonio with me and Linda, and help us get established with a new place to live and a new job. Bernice did a great job keeping the house, cooking meals and taking care of Linda and her own two daughters. My new job required me to represent the company at various projects in south Texas. One of these projects was near Corpus Christi. While there I made contact with Oleen Miller, the married daughter of Mr. and Mrs. Gay. She had been attending church there for some time and had a friend named Frances Ivey who was teaching elementary school in Corpus. Oleen had contacted Frances and me about getting to know each other. Neither Frances nor I was interested in dating. I had not seriously dated, and she was less than anxious to date a man with a two year old child. Finally, out of courtesy to Oleen, I called Frances, and we had a blind date. I was immediately impressed with Frances and she liked me. We continued dating and talked about our situations at length as we drew closer to each other. We met each other's families and discussed every aspect of marriage. Frances and Linda literally embraced each other when they met. Frances holding the daughter she never had, and Linda hugging her mother to be. I have said jokingly that Frances was not sure about marrying me, but when she met Linda, she took me so she could get her.

We were married on September 1, 1956. Shortly after, we agreed that this was a good time for me to start my own consulting business. After a slow start, my work became very profitable as a consulting petroleum engineer while we lived in San Antonio. We were committed to tithe a minimum of 10% of our gross income and increased income gave us the wonderful opportunity to give even more to the Lord's work. We also desired another child, and God blessed us with David on August 2, 1957.

While we were becoming more secure in our finances, we had a growing problem. My work was very demanding and took me to south Texas, west Texas, Louisiana, Alabama, Mississippi, and Montana. This was fine and fun when the children were pre-school age and presented no problem. Frances would put the children in her car and drive to wherever I was working so we could all be together. This became a problem as they grew older and started school. It was not unusual for me to be at a job out of state for two or three weeks at a time, and sometimes more. Frances and I were spiritually uncomfortable with this and began to pray for God to show us a different way. A way to be together more as a family and more active in the local church.

The opportunity came for us to open a tire and automotive repair business in Austin, Texas, with two associates who already had a successful operation at a downtown location. We moved to Austin in August, 1967, and I managed the store. We eventually bought out the other owners and operated the business for the next thirty-five years. On January 7, 1972, we were blessed with another son, Michael. We had been trying to have another child for some time, and Frances used to say that about the time we give up, God will bless us again.

During the early 1980s, Frances sensed that I was missing the challenges of the oil business and she began to pray for God to open a new door for me. At the time, I had turned the store manager position over to my son, David. God answered Frances's prayer and opened an opportunity to go to work as a petroleum engineer with the Texas Railroad Commission (the regulatory agency for oil and gas). I worked there eleven years and earned retirement in 1993. We sold the business and fully retired in 2002.

We loved each other as we walked with God together for fifty-six years. Frances and I had Linda and two wonderful sons, David and

Michael, who loved their mother in a way that brings warmth to my heart. We have seven super grand children and five great grandchildren. Frances died on April 12, 2013, after six months of struggling through the results of a stroke. The two wives God gave me here on Earth were beautiful Christian ladies who loved the Lord and lived for Him while loving me and our family. They now reside with Jesus in heaven.

As God leads, I continue to serve through Great Hills Baptist Church where Frances and I served together for forty-six years. Our most blessed service was as coordinator of the young married adult division and in the men's and women's retreat ministry. We also ministered to older family members who needed us. I currently visit members of our church confined at home, or at assisted living and skilled nursing facilities.

Please understand that these accounts of my life and this book are not about me, but about my Lord Jesus who brought me along the path He planned for me. It is intended to be a testimony of His love, grace, and power; a demonstration of how He could take an ordinary man and use him to His glory.

My journey started when He revealed himself to me and showed me my desperate need for Him. It all began when I admitted that I was a sinner. Romans 3:23 clearly states that we are all sinners doing life our way and not His way. The payment for this sin is death (Romans 6:23). This means spiritual death, eternal, complete separation from God. This same scripture also shows the way out, which is a free gift. Even a free gift must be received as stated in John 1:12. This scripture shows that while I am His creation, I become His child by receiving Jesus who tasted hell for me on the cross. Now I know with certainty that I am a child of God through the free gift Jesus bought and paid for on the cross. I do not hope so, or guess so, I know so. 1 John 5:11 states clearly that he who has Christ has life, and he who does not have Christ does not have life.

You can be just as sure as I am by acting on these simple paths to eternal life. Admit your sin, ask for His forgiveness and receive what Christ did for you as a free gift and become a child of the Creator God. You can know for sure. Do it now.

Establish a relationship with Him by reading from the Scriptures to understand what He is saying to you. Talk to Him in simple prayer everyday and tell Him about yourself and how you feel. He wants to hear from His children even though He already knows all about them. Get into a church that teaches and preaches the Word, so that you may grow into a strong follower of Christ. Pray for God to connect you with a Christian friend that you can share with, and exchange accountability with. We all need a prayer buddy and some one that will confront us with honesty, keeping us accountable in our walk with Christ. If He can use me, He can use you if you let him.

I testify to all who read this that Jesus Christ is God, the Son, who has personally carried me through this life in such a way I can only say, "thank you Lord, I love you."

IF I COULD BE SURE?

LUKE 1:1–4

How many times have you said. "If I could just be sure"? If I could be sure this is the one I should marry; if this is the right job; if this promotion and move is the right thing; if this is the right thing to do with or about my child; if this is the right church; and many times there comes the nagging question, "If I could just be sure of what the Bible says about this."

The Bible very clearly states that the Gospel according to Luke was written to an individual that he might "know for certain" those things in which he had been instructed. Luke very candidly states that there are "many" who have "set forth in hand" those things that are "believed among us" and that there are "eye witnesses" and "ministers of the word." Luke seemed to be compelled to study these accounts of others and write. "In order," the events concerning the Gospel of Christ.

The hard work of Bible study is a matter of fact. Here it is seen that Luke studied the "declaration" of many "eyewitnesses" who wrote "in hand" those things concerning the gospel. No doubt it took a great deal of time to "place it in order" by studying and asking questions of the eyewitnesses. It is also painfully true that Theophilus was going to have to study this writing of Luke and compare it with those things wherein he had been instructed. Then he could be sure.

How do you face indecision? Are the instructions and principles of the Bible stored away in your heart for help at decision-making time? In the Bible God said that you could call on Him and He would show you great and mighty things that you don't know (Jer. 33:3). In 2Timothy 2:15 the Bible says, "study to show thyself approved unto God, a workman that needeth not to be ashamed, rightly dividing the word of truth." How do you call on God? One way is to dust off your Bible and seek Him through His word. Start today and you will learn how to be sure.

THE TIME TO NOT SEEK A SIGN

LUKE 1:5–25

The mother and father of John the Baptist were fine godly people. They were both descendants of Levi, the priestly tribe. Zacharias was even a priest set aside to "execute the priest's office" in the temple. Elizabeth was a descendant of Aaron, Moses' brother, and the first appointed priest for the tabernacle.

However, they had no children, and this was considered a "reproach" and indicated that God may have removed His favor because of sin in their lives. They prayed earnestly to God for a son and kept on walking in the light of the Lord. Then one day as Zacharias was performing his priestly duties, the angel Gabriel told him that Elizabeth would have a son by him and that they should name him John. How wonderful! Their prayer had been answered, but Zacharias did not believe. After all, Elizabeth was too old to have children - but he should have known about Isaac's birth to Sarah and Abraham. Was the birth of Isaac to Sarah in her old age just a Bible story to this man of God, even as many of the examples and stories in the Book are just abstract, powerless accounts of history to us?

Zacharias asked for a sign. There are times not to ask for a sign. When we are not sure of God's direction or if there is confusion about His direction we should be careful to get a word from His Word. But when we pray for something, as Zacharias and Elizabeth did, and God clearly shows us that the prayer will be answered, don't ask for a sign. Receive it and rejoice in it. Are we serious about the things we pray for? Do we look for folks to get saved when we pray for their salvation? Do we wait and watch for a change in the lifestyle of those we pray for? Do we really expect God to hear our prayers and meet us at the point of our need? Look for it. Wait and watch for it and expect it if God has shown us the answers.

Faith Like Mary

Luke 1:26–38

Gabriel was very busy about this time in history, but what a thrilling job he was carrying out for God! He had announced that Elizabeth, the barren wife of Zacharias, would have a son who was to be named John. Now, only six months later, he speaks to Mary about her part in the virgin birth of the Lord Jesus Christ. Someone has said, "Don't you like it when you see a plan come together?" Here we see the plan of God coming together for the final revelation of his redemption program for man. The birth of Jesus is no accident. It is a part of God's beautiful and perfect plan, as we see in the life and ministry of Jesus and John. John was born for the single purpose of preparing the way for Jesus. Jesus was miraculously born of the Virgin Mary for the single purpose of preparing for us a way of salvation so rich and free.

It is interesting to note that Mary did not question the fact of this unbelievable announcement. She was not sure of the greeting expressed by Gabriel, but she quickly received him as who he said he was and she also accepted the purpose for which he came. She did ask the logical question, "How shall this be, seeing I know not a man?" I believe that we should ask God, "How," when he assigns us a difficult and important task. We should ask Him how to do most tasks He assigns us unless the task itself defines the plan for getting it done.

Gabriel very plainly and deliberately explained "How?" and Mary simply said, "be it unto me according to your word," for she recognized that she belonged to the Lord. Oh, that we could and would have the faith of Mary; "be it unto me according to your word, Lord; just give Me the word and the how." Faith is not blind and impulsive. Faith, like Mary's, is based on a word from God and is always followed with obedience and a commitment to get the job done in His power.

CONTINUING FAITH BRINGS AFFIRMATION

LUKE 1:39–45

Mary's faith did not stop or diminish after she accepted Gabriel's announcement to her concerning her part in the birth of Christ. Mary "arose" and went to see Elizabeth, her cousin, whom the angel said was six months pregnant. All she had was a word from God. Now I don't think Mary knew for sure she was pregnant by any physical evidence only a few moments after the miraculous conception took place. All she had was a word from God. If someone asked her where she was going (and they may have), she would have to say that she was going to see her older cousin whom the angel Gabriel told her was six months pregnant, even though she was barren and past the time of child bearing. That's walking in faith based on the word from God!

Walking in faith produced confirmation, for when Mary greeted her cousin, Elizabeth, several things happened to confirm and affirm the ·angel's declaration. First, the baby, John, "leaped" within the womb of Elizabeth. (Notice God's word refers to him as a babe, not a fetus or anything else less than a living, responsive baby). Elizabeth, obviously a godly woman with knowledge of the scriptures concerning the promised Messiah, recognized the affirmation and confirmation of God as she was filled with the Holy Spirit. She did not question the Spirit, but received Him and spoke words of confirmation and encouragement to Mary. Continuing faith brought affirmation.

When we are saved, we receive the Holy Spirit who lives in us from then on. Our problem is that we don't "receive" Him as a welcome, desirable part of everyday life. This grieves Him and makes His power ineffective in our lives. We, like Mary, must walk in faith based on a word from God out of the Word of God about specific matters, honoring the dear Holy Spirit in the process. Then we must continue to walk in faith looking forward to affirmation by a loving, caring God.

Spontaneous Praise To God

Luke 1:46–56

Mary probably didn't feel pregnant, but she was carrying the "Seed of Woman" spoken of in Genesis. Elizabeth shouldn't be expecting at her age, but she was six months pregnant with John the Baptist. The angel Gabriel had spoken impossible things to both of these woman but they were true. Mary had submitted to the word from God, walked in faith to visit cousin Elizabeth, and now as the magnitude of the reality of these events unfolded in her heart, she burst out with spontaneous praise to God!

How beautiful to see this young Hebrew girl pluck from her mind and heart, with the help of the Holy Spirit, bits of scripture and possibly excerpts from her father's prayers, or perhaps those of cousin Zacharias, and then speak so that history could record this beautiful praise. Who is man that God should consider him? Yet He has made us "a little lower than the angels" and involves Himself in the everyday things of our lives. Mary recognized this and praised and worshipped Him.

We can and should enjoy this same fellowship with God the Father through Jesus Christ our Lord and the dear Holy Spirit. If we are in the Word daily, praying through circumstance by circumstance, humbling ourselves under the mighty hand of God, we too will have this type of fellowship. As circumstances come up in the normal routine of our life, the Word will come up from our mind and heart as the Holy Spirit applies it to these situations, and we will experience God involving Himself in the little routine things of our life. We receive this fellowship and walk by faith based on His Word and then affirmation comes. Spontaneous praise and worship must follow. Who are we that You, God, should even consider us? Yet, You have chosen to love us enough to save us and then fellowship with us on a personal, intimate basis: Oh Lord our God, How Great Thou Art!

MERCY, OBEDIENCE, AND ANOINTING

LUKE 1:57–66

Childbearing is difficult, at best, just like God said it would be as He spoke to Eve in the Garden after the fall of man. It usually becomes more difficult with age but in Elizabeth's case it was so easy for her that it made the local news. Her "neighbors" and cousin heard about it and were amazed. How accurately this was attributed to God's mercy, but isn't it true that God's mercy always accompanies his demands on us? A beautiful principle woven in the scriptures is simply that God will provide the grace and mercy for us to do that which He commands us to do.

When the time came to name the child, Elizabeth was obedient to God's direction that he be named John. Some said this was unusual since none of the kinfolk were named John. That's like saying, "Maybe you missed God," or "Are you sure this is what God said?" When they motioned to papa Zacharias, he wrote down the name John and immediately he could speak. It was extremely important that they be obedient to God's word for them concerning the child. It would have been easy to forget or at least de-emphasize the importance of obedience; after all, the impact of the miracle was over after nine months of pregnancy. Maybe this was an unusual but natural phenomena. But wait, don't we do just that? God speaks or delivers us and we drift away from His divine touch and settle for a natural but unusual explanation. We must be obedient to God's revelation completely and totally. Notice that Zacharias did not speak when the child was born but only after he personally wrote the name John.

God was glorified and fear came on all the people, for they knew God was in it all the way. Then last and greatest came the anointing as God's hand was with him. His anointing will follow with us also as we obey His word. Our greatest need is to obey all the Word we know, not to know all the Word.

A Prophet With A new Message

Luke 1:67–80

Zacharias has not been able to speak for at least nine months, and now that God has freed his tongue, he comes forth with a beautiful prophecy about Jesus and his own son, John the Baptist.

First, he recalls and praises God for the blessings of the past, for the great blessing of the now, and for the visitation to "raise up a horn of salvation in the house of David," even Jesus. He then makes a panoramic review of that which was spoken by the prophets of old; of that which describes the expanding, progressive unfolding of the plan of God. This shows that the most significant blessing of God toward "Old Israel" was to save them from their enemies and from the hand of those who hated them, thereby honoring the covenant made with Abraham. Being thus free from the hand of their enemies, they could serve God in holiness and righteousness thereby showing the world the great Salvation of God.

Then Zacharias moves to his son, John, and clearly speaks of the plan and purpose for his life. He is to "go before" the Lord Jesus Christ to "prepare His ways" showing that the way to Him is by the remission of sin. The day longed for and looked toward is now come! The promised Messiah has been born and John is a new prophet with the message. Salvation is now shown clearly and plainly to be on a personal basis. Each one enlightened that he may come out of darkness into the light of Jesus; from the shadow of death to the light of life.

John was true to his calling. He paid the price of obedience to God's anointing. Jesus said of him that he was the greatest of all men born of women. He humbled himself and was totally submissive to the spoken will of God, even though his own father was the spokesman. How many young people will receive the admonition of godly parents today? Those who do, grow strong in spirit, and they, too, become prophets with a living message to a wicked and perverse generation.

WITNESS AND BLESSING BY SUBMISSION

LUKE 2:1–7

I can't remember ever being summoned for jury duty when it was convenient. The preparation of my annual income tax is always at a bad time. More importantly, I think a few unwholesome words sometimes grump forth from my mouth, and those around me witness that I react just like everybody else. This should not be. The greatest time to show Christ in control is when submission to authority is most difficult.

Mary and Joseph give us a good example of submission to governmental authority even though it was a silly law of taxation which came at the worst possible time for them personally. In our day the doctor will hardly let us travel long distances during the last month of pregnancy even with the most modern means of transportation - surely not on a donkey. Could it be that Mary and Joseph knew that nothing could happen to this child? After all, the angel Gabriel had brought word from God, and there was no way possible that anything could prevent His birth. So they left in faith, continuing to walk in faith on the word and authority of God's direction. As things became more difficult, they did not cry to God or get angry with Him. They just kept walking in the light provided and received every obstacle as an opportunity for God to do His will through their submission. The result was the birth of Jesus Christ the Lord, just as it had been prophesied in days of old.

How about us? I'm afraid that we gripe and grump and resist the providence of God by active resistance to the authority applied to our lives. God "resists the proud but gives grace to the humble." The Bible teaches that we should submit to all authority, and the blessing of a good witness will result. To be submissive to authority when it hurts is obvious to those about us. Doors of opportunity to share a witness for Him are opened that cannot be opened by any other key.

Good News For Everyone

Luke 2:8–20

George Washington is for Americans, Napoleon is for the French, and each country has its own heroes. Many of these men and women came from royal, aristocratic backgrounds, but some came from the pits of the poor and this makes the admiration of their accomplishments even more heart warming.

Jesus, the Son of God, was born to the poor in difficult times, and the first to receive the announcement were the shepherds. This good news was not restricted to the palace of the king or the religious leaders of the temple. In fact, they were to be the last to hear - but they did hear.

The good news of Jesus Christ is for everyone. That's what "Gospel" means - good news! God seems to work in a way that the least likely are the very ones to be used. David, the youngest, most insignificant of Jesse's boys was chosen to slay the giant and become King of Judah. Joseph, the obscure son of Jacob, hated by his brothers, was used of God to show the results of the power of God in a man yielded to His will. No matter what our station in life, no matter our race or gender, no matter when or where we are in history - the good news of Christ is for us and if we heed this good news, we are sure to be changed.

The big question is, what will we do with it once we receive it? The shepherds left their flocks and went immediately to see Jesus. Once they had seen Him they told everybody that would listen (they made known abroad). What about you? Have you heard and received or have you heard and rejected? Surely you've heard! What about you? Once you've heard, did you make it known in the circle where you live? We should make it known once we've received for this is truly good news for everyone! Ask God to give you the opportunity to share the good news with someone today.

TRUTH REVEALED

LUKE 2:21–40

Have you ever driven along and seen objects or images formed by the clouds? You are looking and all of a sudden it takes shape in your mind, but when you try to describe and show it to someone else they cannot see it. I had this problem with some of the heavier math as an associate or instructor tried to explain the process of solving a problem. Then suddenly it took shape and it was seen, completely and simply with the patient guidance of another.

This story which records a day of history in the life of Jesus speaks to the truth being revealed by the Holy Spirit. The child Jesus had been seen by many from the time of His birth at Bethlehem but not many truly recognized Him for who He really was. The truth of the matter is that no one can recognize Jesus for who He really is except by the patient guidance of the Holy Spirit. We can drive beneath the clouds for endless hours oblivious to the images formed by them until someone points out the formation and patiently shows it to us.

We can also recognize those objects in the sky, or solve problems effectively by practice and consistency. Notice that Simon and Anna were devout servants of God. They had read in the Scriptures and heard the teaching and preaching about the promised Messiah so that when the Spirit showed them truth they recognized it. These folks had walked with God through the years by faith until they came to the point that they could and would receive the revelation of a deeper truth.

I heard Adrian Rogers say once that light acted upon brings more light and light rejected brings more darkness. It all starts with revelation of The Truth (JESUS) and the action of receiving Him as Lord and Savior. Then life becomes a journey of continuing revelation as we read the Word and fellowship with Him under the patient guidance of the dear Holy Spirit.

GROWTH BY HUMILTY

LUKE 2:41–52

There were times as a child when my parental authority erred, and I made mistakes that were disturbing to me. There have been many times since, when my boss, my pastor or some other authority erred in the handling of a situation. Many times my response has been to rise up with indignation or even hostility. In short, my pride made me resent such error, and I acted with rejection of this incompetent authority.

The Bible plainly teaches that we are to submit to the authority placed over us for it is established by God for our protection and for His plan. In this account of "Jesus in the temple" we see the Son of God displaying great wisdom at the age of twelve as He expounds on the Scripture, which were probably exposed to Him by His earthly parents. His knowledge and wisdom captured the doctors of theology while his parents were probably horrified because they did not know where He was.

Perhaps they should have been more careful in keeping up with His whereabouts, but the thing that is most impressive about this account is that the Son of God moved from being about the business of His Heavenly Father to this position of submission to the authority of His earthly parents. He humbled Himself under the mighty hand of God that He might be exalted in due time. It was not a matter of who was right or wrong, it was a matter of obedience to the Scriptures He knew and understood so well, "children, obey your parents." The closing note is that He "increased in wisdom and stature and favor with God and man." He grew by humility.

The Bible says, "Let this mind be in you which was also in Christ Jesus... who humbled Himself...." We need to grow by humility, and one of the best ways is to submit to authority. God resists the proud but gives grace to the humble.

BEAR FRUIT WHERE YOU ARE

LUKE 3:1–14

It had been a long, long time since the days of the Old Testament when God's prophets and kings spoke a word from God to the people of Israel. Now comes John the Baptist, the one written of by Isaiah, saying that he would come as a voice crying in the wilderness, "Prepare ye the Way of the Lord." John had one purpose in life and that was to humbly prepare the way for Jesus to come upon the scene of history as the promised Messiah. He did it so well that Jesus said that he was the greatest born of woman.

John's message was simply repent, get right with God and get ready for the coming Messiah. He blew one of the theories of that day to be a child of Abraham was enough to be right with God. Not so different from our day. To be a church member; to come from a "good family;" to tip our hat to God on occasion; to be a citizen of a "Christian nation" or a member of a "Christian family" – this is not enough. It is nothing in the light of Jesus. Jesus said that unless we repent, we should all likewise perish.

This message of John brought people out from all walks of life. Their question of him was the same, "What must I do?" His answer was the same to all: bear fruit where you are - "Bring forth fruit worthy of repentance." Repentance means not only to be sorry, but to change your ways. As one preacher says, "Let your walk match your talk." To the "people" he answered that they must share with others and be compassionate. To the publicans he said be fair and honest in your dealings with people. To the soldiers he said be content with your pay and treat people with justice and fairness. He told none of them to change professions, but to simply bear fruit where they were.

That is God's message to us today. If your profession or job is honorable, be satisfied with it and bear fruit for God. Be all God wants you to be where you are. "Bear fruit where you are."

HUMILITY EXEMPLIFIED

LUKE 3:15–22

One of the most difficult areas of the Christian life is humility, yet it seems to be the most important. The Bible admonishes us to have the same mind as Jesus - one of humility. The opposite of this is pride, that trait and character that brings us to say that we have our rights. Our inner being boils up with such thoughts as "I don't deserve to be treated like this," "I work harder than they do, but I never get recognition;" "Why should I be asked to do the dirty work all the time?" and on and on - my rights, my feelings, my position. Yet the Bible says that we are to humble ourselves under the mighty hand of God. Jesus said, "He that loses his life for my sake will save it." Again, the Bible says that we are not to think more of ourselves than we should, rather we are to put others first. The Lord still resists the proud and gives grace to the humble.

In the account of John's response as to whether or not he was the Messiah, he did not brag about being the forerunner for the Christ but simply and humbly said, "One mightier than I cometh, the latchet of whose shoes I am not worthy to unloose..." He continued to lift up Jesus and put himself down. How easy it is for us to lead the conversation away from Jesus and toward our "belief" about this or that subject-away from what He has done for us to what we have done for Him.

We also see in this same account, Jesus humbling himself to be baptized by John. What an example of humility! The King of Kings, Lord of Lords, the great Creator comes to be baptized by John! Maybe He left us this example knowing how much we would resist actions of humility in our own lives. Let us exemplify humility. It is the example of our Lord, and it is a source of God's grace that seems to be ever present. We need to concentrate on humbling ourselves and leave it to God to exalt us, if and when He sees fit to do so.

THE GOD OF PEOPLE

LUKE 3:23–38

How many of us can name our great grandparents? How about our great, great or great, great, great grandparents! In this scripture, Luke accounts for the ancestors of Jesus all the way back to Adam. Luke was not even related to the folks, but God revealed it to him though the Holy Spirit by the account of others or perhaps by written documents. Suffice it to say God knew those folks by name all the way back to Adam. Our God is a God of people, individuals personally important to Him.

God keeps good records. It is amazing that this record of the lineage of Jesus' earthly father, Joseph, was available. God had it all put away for the proper time to show that His Word, spoken by the prophets of old, was accurate. His Word predicted long, long ago that Jesus the Christ would be born of the tribe of Judah of the seed of David. Even the wicked King Herod determined from the Scriptures where this predicted King would come from. From his trust in the accuracy of this word, he had the children of Bethlehem killed in attempt to destroy Jesus.

God keeps perfect, detailed records about each of us even today, but His most important record is what we have done with Jesus. That record supersedes all other records, and our individual name may be placed in this "Lamb's Book of Life" by receiving Jesus as "the Way," "the Truth," "the Life," "the Son of God" - our hope, our salvation. God so loves us, individually, by name, that He sent Jesus to pay for our sins that we may repent and receive Him as our only Lord and Savior. Our God is the God of people - no one is excluded and no one is preferred —Jesus died for all!

If we had a relative listed in Luke's account of the ancestors of Jesus, we would hurry through the list to proudly point out the names of our forefathers. Much more important is that our own name be listed in the "Lamb's Book of Life." Yet so many don't seem to care. Is your name there? Have you checked it out?

TEMPTATION IS SEASONAL

LUKE 4:1–15

The farmer's business is seasonal. There is a time to plant and a time to harvest each crop. There is a time to feed and a time to market certain livestock. Most retail businesses are seasonal. Certain things sell better in winter, or spring, or at Christmas time or at the beginning of school. One thing you can count on, the season will return again and again and again.

The closing words of this account of the temptation of Jesus says "...he (the devil) departed from Him for a season." He came back, for sure, on many occasions, but Jesus continued to be "without sin." He was tempted is every way like we are tempted. We don't always think so, for we are like the hang-glider struggling at 500 feet unaware of the jet liner streaking overhead at 35,000 feet. However, that jet liner had to take off just like the hang-glider and pass through the critical altitude of 500 feet before it reached its cruising altitude.

So it is with us, I think, as we struggle with the temptation of pride, or fear, or jealously or whatever. We feel that no one, not even Jesus, has been tried like this. However, in this account, we see Him in great hunger, and alone for forty days without family or friends. At this point, the devil reminded Him that the things of the flesh are at hand - things that satisfy the desire of the flesh. Jesus said that there are things more important - the word of God - His fellowship with the Father. The devil said that power, unbelievable power, was available if Jesus would just compromise and worship him. Not so, said Jesus, God is first in my life, and that is more important than pride. Then came the opportunity for spiritual show-off, a chance to show the folks how spiritual you are! Not so, said Jesus, God doesn't need any help in this area. The devil left for a season, but he came back and he'll be back at us - be ready! Be prepared like Jesus, who had a close personal relationship with the Father and a commitment to live by the Word.

SEEING IS BELIEVING

LUKE 4:16–29

It's so easy to explain and expound on a truth from the Scriptures once we have been enlightened. Not only is it easy, but it is fun and exciting to discuss revelation received from God's Word. Strangely enough, there are times when our explanation of this new found revelation rolls off the ears of those we try to persuade. Many times the only way they will believe is to see what we are in our personal walk relative to our new-found truth.

Jesus read a passage written hundreds of years before and told the people in His own hometown that this scripture spoke of Him. They were most impressed, and He knew it. Then He spoke of the day of His persecution and crucifixion, planting a seed in their minds. He simply said that they would see Him suffer and say to Him, "Physician, heal thyself." No doubt, many of these people believed after they saw His suffering, His anointed attitude, and His victory over death. We know for sure that it changed the lives of certain members of His earthly family. Seeing was believing for James and other members of the family.

Many of the lives we touch ponder our words of witness, see us as we pray and hear us as we read the Scriptures. Some may even be under our teaching in a Bible study situation. The truth, however, is that most of these lives will not be deeply influenced by what we say until they see a victory in our lives. Unfortunately, this victory must be preceded with difficulty in order to reach maximum impact. The devil told God that it was not surprising for Job to serve Him because he was so blessed of God. What would he do under the pressure of difficulty? Seeing is believing, the devil said, and he is still saying this to those we try to influence for God.

The real question is, how do we receive difficulty and how do we respond to adversity? Do we moan and groan or do we receive it as an opportunity to drive home a truth we are speaking with a life we are living? Remember, seeing is believing. The world demands it, and so do we.

POWER COMES FROM PRESSURE

LUKE 4:30–37

Watch the weight lifter and see the veins on his neck bulge as he strains against the pressure of the weights. The muscles grow and tighten as he works out day after day. Without the pressure and persistence, this would not happen.

This same principle holds true in our spiritual power and growth. There can be little growth without the pressure: difficult decisions that drive us to our knees and into the Word; temptation to criticize or murmur gossip or demand our own way. The weakness of an insensitive spirit will cause us to overlook a hurting humanity and fail to see the fate of the lost about us. The weakness of our ever-present pride brings us to evaluate all things against how it makes us look. These weaknesses will grow to be a way of life making us ineffective for Christ unless we are brought under pressure to seek God's solution. This process of spiritual weightlifting develops the strength and power of our inner spirit to overcome these ever-present weak spots in our lives.

It is not without significance that Jesus had been tempted of the devil for forty days just prior to the exhibition of spiritual power recorded in this passage. Note the following:

1. He passed through the midst of them and went His way. (Power to stand alone for right without being offensive.)

2. He came and taught and they were astonished, for His Word was with power. (Power to teach the Word.)

3. Jesus rebuked the unclean devil after he had recognized Him. (The power to expose the devil and the power to live the kind of life that frightens the devil.)

4. Fame went out about His authority and power. (The power to walk and talk a powerful persistent life that gets the attention of the world.)

Lord, give us stress and pressure that we might be perfected and made into the powerful person you want us to be.

HEALING OF PEOPLE GOD'S WAY

LUKE 4:38–44

Divine healing is viewed in different ways by different people. Some say it is based strictly on faith, no faith - no healing; or not enough faith for healing. The big question with this is how much faith does it take and whose faith is required: the faith of the sick or the faith of the one praying for the sick? How much faith does it take to be saved? Does is take more faith to be healed of a temporal bodily ailment or a terminal spiritual death?

Some say that divine healing is slow and gradual. "Name it and claim it" and just keep on saying it day after day, and the sickness will gradually go away. Others say all healing is divine with some healing being miraculous as it pleases God to perform such healing.

There is certainly divine healing, in that, we are His creation and created within us is the healing process. Doctors study these processes and provide the best possible healing situation for our body. It is also obvious that God is sovereign and heals whom He pleases. Who could have more faith than Paul, yet he was not healed. God had something for Paul that would glorify Him more.

In this passage we see Jesus healing Peter's mother-in-law. We see that this healing was miraculous and instant, not gradual. In the other case Jesus healed "everyone" of them with no mention of a faith check. How much faith can someone have with a devil in them? Yet we see that "devils also came out of many."

God is sovereign. Who can know the mind of God? Who is man that He would consider us - His ways are high above ours. Job's attempt to know the ways of God caused him to be ashamed and humiliated. God has built into our bodies a healing process, with which we should cooperate. He also miraculously heals. We should come to Him with the measure of faith that we have, requesting that He consider our case or the case of a friend or loved one and leave the results to Him.

THE PERSONAL TOUCH

LUKE 5:1–11

Has Jesus ever touched you personally? Have you ever labored with a problem or a difficult decision and had Him show you the way? Or perhaps you were just minding your own business when He reached out and touched you.

Peter had just heard the message that Jesus had spoken to the crowd. He could hardly miss it since Jesus was delivering the message from Peter's boat. After the speaking was over, Jesus asked them to take the boat out to the deep and drop the nets for fish. These men had fished all night without a catch, and they were experts. There must have been something in Jesus' message or perhaps a personal relationship was established, for they did what their non-fishing friend said.

The results were unbelievable. The catch was so great that nets began to break and the boats began to sink under the load of the fish that were caught. Jesus had touched Peter and these men as they witnessed a miracle expressed in a dimension that they understood; a touch designed to change their lives. Then Jesus gave an invitation to live in the experience of His touch. "Come follow me and I will make you fishers of men." Following Jesus then became the number one priority of their lives, and fishing for men became a part of their everyday life.

Jesus stands ready and eager to show Himself strong on your behalf so that you, too, may experience His personal touch and put Him first in your life. Look for His touch in business decisions, personal commitments, home building, child raising, being a good husband or wife. When you see and feel His touch, do as Peter did. Bow before Him, humble yourself and acknowledge His wonderful grace and power by making Him number one in your life.

THE HEALING TOUCH

LUKE 5:12–15

It seems that it is never convenient to reach out and touch another person when they are hurting. It requires so much time and commitment. We have so much already in motion and so many projects already going that another commitment of our time seems impossible. And besides, it probably won't be just a single touch but an ongoing obligation to wade through the slow healing process.

The lack of commitment to this process of sharing and giving a healing touch comes from the lack of true compassion and obedience to our Lord's command. "Love the Lord thy God and love your neighbor as yourself," Jesus said, and then He gave the story of the "Good Samaritan" as an example of who our neighbor really is. The good news is that when we commit our time to reach out to the hurting with a healing touch, God blesses and we are able to experience a new joy in ministering alongside Him.

Jesus reached out to touch one "full of leprosy." How disgusting! This outcast was afflicted with the epitome of unsightly diseases. This disease was considered so contagious that its victims were separated and placed apart to suffer their affliction in isolation with other victims. Yet Jesus reached out with the healing touch. His compassion for this helpless, hopeless, hurting human who lay humbly at His feet overcame all reservations and reasons not to help.

Jesus not only healed the leper but also taught him a way to follow that would give a good witness to others. This is usually true when we, too, reach out. For we find the opportunity to share Jesus, as the Word, the Way, the Life, the true touch of healing for the soul.

COMPLETE HEALING BY JESUS

LUKE 5:16–26

Winston Churchill admonished a group during World War II to never give up, never, never, never give up. If this is good counsel for a people engaged in the struggle for survival in the midst of a world war, why not for the Christian soldier engaged in the battles of life for his Lord?

The friends of the sick man had this kind of attitude. They would not be deterred. They were determined to bring their friend to Jesus. The motive for their determination was faith that Jesus could help their friend.

We give up too easily. How many times do we resolve to pray for a relative, a friend or an associate only to be stunned by some reminder months or years later that we not only failed to continue to pray but totally forgot the commitment? How often have we determined to take someone into our life and minister Christ to them until they could stand alone, only to see them fall through the crack as we become caught up in other things? Never give up, never, never, never.

It is worth the effort, for Jesus heals completely. Not only is He able to heal the body, but more importantly, He heals the spirit and the soul in the act of complete healing. It seems that we sometimes get more excited over the healing of the body, which is temporal, than the healing of the spirit, which is eternal. What is more important, that disease be removed or that sins be forgiven?

In this case Jesus said, "Their sins are forgiven," thereby reaching far beyond the man's physical needs to his spiritual needs. The purpose of this was to show the Pharisees, and us, that Jesus not only has the power and authority to heal the body but can reach into the soul and forgive sins. With this power available to us as Christians through prayer, the Word, and obedience, we should never give up on those who are spiritually sick but continue to look to Jesus in faith for their complete healing.

REACHING OUTSIDE

LUKE 5:27–32

Statistics show that those in a church fellowship have fewer friends outside the church the longer they remain as active members. When they are first saved and become a church member, they know a number of folks outside the church on an intimate basis. They play golf, play bridge, shop, talk on the phone regularly and enjoy many other forms of friendly communication. Then the number of their friendships outside begins to diminish, and the number of friends inside the church begins to increase. It is also a fact that the higher the position of leadership in the church the fewer outside friends we have. The pastor and his wife have the least number of outside friends, statistically.

This is not the way Jesus meant for us to be after we are saved and have made Him Lord of our lives. Jesus said, in effect, "You are to be in this world but not of this world." Someone has pointed out that if the only reason we are saved is to go to heaven, then why doesn't God take us home the moment we are saved? The answer is shown by Jesus in the calling of Levi. This example is repeated over and over by Jesus as He reached outside the religious bunch and His own followers to touch the lives of the outsiders.

Jesus was sensitive to the potential of Levi, the tax collector, the hated outcast who took taxes from his countrymen for the ruthless Roman government which occupied the land. Levi was so grateful for the opportunity to follow Jesus that he threw a party and invited his lost friends to meet Jesus.

That is our job and calling. Jesus left us here to reach out beyond the walls of the church, and to do that we must establish meaningful relationships. "Go ye therefore and teach all nations." All of us touch the lives of outsiders every day. We work with them, we buy from them, their kids go to school with ours, they are everywhere. We must be sensitive to their presence and show them the way to peace with Jesus.

WHOSE DISCIPLE ARE WE?

LUKE 5:33–39

The scribes and Pharisees had just questioned the socializing of Jesus and His disciples with sinners. Now they questioned why Jesus' disciples did not fast and pray like the disciples of John the Baptist and those of the Pharisees. To this, Jesus pointed out that there was no need to fast since He was with them.

John the Baptist and the Pharisees were looking forward to the coming Messiah. John was enlightened and recognized Jesus as the promised One, and he recognized that his task was to make ready for His ministry. The Pharisees were blind, for the most part, as to who Jesus was. It was common in that day to put on clothes of sack material, pour ashes over one's head and fast and pray. Even today they go to the Wailing Wall in Jerusalem and pray for the Messiah to come. Jesus was saying that He was the promised One, and there was no need for fasting and praying. The time was for rejoicing and proclaiming the good news.

So it is today. One that is without Jesus should come to the point of humbly praying for salvation, or his loved ones and friends should be praying and fasting on his behalf. But those who know Him as Lord and Savior should be rejoicing, celebrating and proclaiming the good news.

There are some who attach themselves to those who teach Old Testament doctrine without applying the truth revealed in the New Testament. They become like the Pharisees of old, always "preparing for" His coming or always "adding to" the sufficiency of His presence. They are trying to get the wineskins of the Old Testament law to hold the new wine of God's grace through Jesus Christ. They are trying to patch Jesus and His free gift of salvation into the worn cloth of the Old Testament law.

Jesus is Lord and we become His disciples when we receive Him as Savior and Lord. He is all we need, for "old things are passed away, behold all things are become new." (II Cor. 5:17). Let us pursue Him with victory in our lives, not with sackcloth and ashes. After all, whose disciples are we?

LAW OR LOVE; BOND OR FREE

LUKE 6:1–11

The Pharisees were more interested in the letter of the law than the latitude of love. They watched the disciples of Jesus as they pulled corn in the fields as they traveled on the Sabbath. They watched Jesus like a hawk to see what He would do with the Sabbath, and they missed what He did for the people and what He wanted to do for them.

They were hostile over the healing of a helpless man while they could have been happy over the power that revealed the Prince of Peace. There was no question in their minds that He could heal, for the Scripture says that they, "...watched Him whether He would heal on the Sabbath day; that they might find an accusation against Him." They put the law over love and remained bound when they could have been free.

Do we sometimes get so caught up in the legality of the issue that we miss the joy in the experience? Do we make Sunday (the Lord's Day, the first day of the week) a day of rest and an opportunity of worship and praise to our Lord? Has Sunday become a rigid day of form and order of worship, with the only satisfaction from our trip to the church house being that we went through the motions? Do we come home from church on Sunday and chalk up another duty accomplished?

What is it like at work and in our everyday lives? Do we watch and nitpick the behavior of the those about us and fail to recognize the love and fellowship of our Lord that is available to us? It seems that sometimes all we can see is the faults in others, and we lose sight of Jesus. I have found a good solution to this. It is simply to pray about the faults I see in others and ask God to help others see and correct these faults. In the same breath, I pray that He will reveal the truth about these same faults in my own life and give me victory. This makes me more lovable than legal and helps free me from the bondage of criticism.

Pray And Pick

Luke 6:12–19

When we live with a problem, a circumstance, or an opportunity for a long time, we tend to make our decisions as a natural matter of course based on our human assessment. It would be interesting at this point to recall and list all the decisions that turned out to be wrong, that caused us much stress, that at best had many rough spots, and that we wish we had never made in the way we did. These bad decisions are behind us now and there is nothing we can do about most of them. We can prepare for future decisions and get help in making them.

Jesus shows a great principle that we should all apply to our lives. Pray about every decision, and pray until you get an answer. The Lord had lived with those from whom He would choose the twelve apostles and could have made a good pick based on His personal knowledge of them. This was not good enough for our Lord and should not be good enough for us. He prayed all night over this decision and then went out the next morning and made the pick based on the prayer. Surely Jesus was in an attitude of prayer all the time, for His Book says "pray without ceasing." He applied another scriptural admonition that is to be careful for nothing, but in all things make our wishes known in prayer and thanksgiving. He prayed before he picked.

We, too, must pray without ceasing. We must have a regular time to read the Scriptures and pray about specific people with specific needs and about specific problems and opportunities. We must then walk through each day in an attitude of prayer about these people and things, being sensitive to new opportunities and people we need to pray for "without ceasing." But when we have a big decision to make we need to "go apart" and pray until we get an answer. We need to pray and then pick, not pick and then pray for God to bless our decision.

REPROACH AND REWARD

LUKE 6:20–26

Recently, I was counseling with a person going through a divorce, and this person was ready to give in to the pressure and agree to anything to avoid the hassle. He had just recently become a Christian and was very sensitive about doing what God wanted him to do. A Christian marriage counselor had shown him where it was not God's will for divorce and that the Scriptures indicate that God hates divorce. He was advised to resist the divorce, seek his wife's forgiveness, and commit to a position that he would never willingly become divorced. This caused much pressure from his wife and even brought the threat of an ugly divorce proceeding in which his errors of the past were bound to surface.

What's the difference? Was not a divorce inevitable, either by agreement or by the wife's filing? The difference was obedience, even at reproach, knowing that the reward of God's pleasure toward obedience at all cost was sufficient. Too many times our actions are based on what people will think, not what God has told us to do in His Word.

In this scriptural account of Jesus teaching His disciples, He encouraged them to take the stand for Him. He assured them that the reward later for the reproach of the present is more than worth it. He also pointed out that if people are speaking well of us and we are most satisfied in the things of the world, we are in danger. Usually the more reasonable our action is from a human point of view, the more likely it is to be contrary to God's way.

The danger is in getting reward and reproach mixed up. What is better, the reward of men and the reproach of God or the reward of God and the reproach of men? Take a stand of obedience to God's Word and His plan for your life. It will bring reproach from some, but more importantly, it will bring reward from God.

THE "DO GOOD" ATTITUDE

LUKE 6:27–36

Most of our "do good" attitudes are hinged to the attitudes of those to whom we do good. If we like them, we desire to do good to them. If they do good to us, we desire to do good to them. If it will make us look good or benefit our standing, we desire to do good to them. Of course this is not always true, but it is certainly the tendency. This is the natural way, but the scriptures warn that there is a way which "seems right" to man but its end is the way of death.

Jesus presents a most disturbing admonition in this scripture. Can we love our enemies, do good to those who hate us, give without expecting in return and lend without hope of gain? Of course this admonition must be taken in the light of other scriptures which say that if a man doesn't work he doesn't eat, or that we are to work six days and rest one, or that which admonishes us to behold the ant as he works hard and orderly.

The key here is the admonition to be merciful. This tells us not to give as one deserves but to give as we are able and as we have opportunity placed before us by God. This means that we must consider the brother who is not worthy because he wastes that which he has. We must get our lives involved in his so as to teach him how to take care of that which he has, teach him how to earn, how to save, how to experience the joy of giving back to God and others in need. The truth is we would rather give money and forget it than give money or goods combined with our time in an effort to discipline the one in need.

God is merciful to us. We don't get what we deserve and sometimes not even what we want. We get something much better as He gives us His personal attention focused toward making us become what we should be in time. This is the real "do good" attitude expressed by our Lord toward us every day of our lives. Should our "do good" attitude toward those about us be any different?

MOTES, BEAMS, AND PRAYERS

LUKE 6:37–42

Why does God allow us to see a "splinter" in a fellow Christian's life if He doesn't want us to pull it out? Like other Christians, I have been "blessed" with the ability to see many faults in others while thinking that I am near perfect. I have been known to see error in my pastor's life, my wife and children's lives, my boss's life and on and on. The human tendency is to take it upon oneself to point out these errors and give good sound advice for corrections. The only problem with this is that it does not work, and the reason it does not work is because it is against the admonition of our Lord as recorded in the Word. As Ron Dunn says, "the only problem with this is that it's wrong."

It's obvious from the Scripture that the brother has a flaw (mote); and the observer has a flaw (beam); it is obvious that neither can lead the other out in this condition (blind leading the blind); and it is also obvious that there is a clear way to take care of both. It appears that the only solution is in prayer. Could it be that God has shown us a flaw in a brother's life as a call from God for us to pray on his behalf? Could it be that God wants us to always look in and search for errors in our own life when He reveals a flaw in a brother's life to us?

I am learning to respond in prayer when God gives me the insight to see a mote in a fellow Christian's eye. My prayer goes like this: "Lord, you have shown me this error in my brother's life. By this you have alerted me that there could be a bigger error in my own life. You have also alerted me to pray for this brother and for myself. Show him this error and if I am to help, please give me the opportunity to counsel without offense. Just in case the error is with me, apply the same pressure to my spirit that I am asking you to apply to his, so that I may confess and follow you toward perfection." We grow in forgiveness and humility by motes, beams and prayers.

THE HEART: A SOURCE OF FRUIT

LUKE 6:43–45

There are beautiful trees and bushes in nature which produce fruit that is deadly. There are also ugly plants that produce delicious fruit. The watermelon and cantaloupe vines run along the ground and are hardly something one would plant in the flower bed at home. The melon itself is an unattractive thing, but when it is cut open, its meat is beautiful and delicious. The deadly plant cannot produce a delicious melon and the melon vine cannot produce deadly fruit. This is because of something within its system that produces the same fruit every time.

There are attractive people who are forever critical of others, of situations and circumstances. There are plain and ordinary folks who are uplifting, encouraging and productive. Each of these groups simply expresses that which is built into their system; it comes from their heart. Neither group can produce the fruit of the other without a change of heart. The Bible says that there would come a time when God will write the law on the hearts of the people. The Bible says that the heart is desperately wicked and who can know it, but it also says that in Jesus all things can be made new, even the heart.

The truth spoken by our Lord in this scripture show that the mouth is the avenue from which the fruit comes. Even as a delicious melon is cut open to expose the beautiful sweet meat, the mouth comes open and words come forth from the heart. A wicked heart produces wicked words, and a renewed heart full of Jesus produces beautiful words of truth. The heart is a source of fruit which is produced through the mouth. All the fruit inspector has to do is monitor the words that come forth, whether they be sweet, uplifting, edifying, hostile, unwholesome, or depressing. The Bible says that we are to let no unwholesome word come out of our mouth, but only words that are good for edification according to the need of the moment so that they might minister grace to those who hear (Eph. 4: 29). Do the words of our mouth which come from the meditations of our heart minister God's grace to those who hear?

TO DO OR NOT TO DO, THAT IS THE QUESTION

LUKE 6:46–49

In this discourse, Jesus dealt with the most fundamental problem of human beings: to do or not to do that which one knows one should do. To be obedient to those in authority over us or not. To carry out the orders and directions or not. These are the questions, and it boils down to our everyday life.

The Bible admonishes children to obey their parents in the Lord, and to this, every Christian parent says, "Amen." The Bible says that every worker should be obedient to his employer, and to this every manager says, "Amen." The Bible says that we are to be obedient to the civil authority placed over us, including rendering the tax to "Caesar," but to this we sometimes say, "No Amen." Jesus says in this scripture very clearly that we are to do what He says if we call him Lord. To make Jesus Lord of our lives is simply to do what He says all the time, in all situations.

Jesus compares this basic truth to building a house founded on obedience or disobedience; there is no other option offered. Partial obedience is like a foundation with holes in it that will ultimately cause the entire foundation to crack and fail. To stand firm in life, we must know what the Bible says about life's problems and then be obedient to these teachings.

Our lives are like houses, and they are each built on one of these two foundations: to do what the Book says or not do what the Book says, that is the question. Notice Jesus did not say "if" the storms come but "when" the storms come. The storms of life will come and whether or not we stand depends on our foundation. The storms of financial difficulty, family conflicts, marital stresses, child-raising, secular job problems, health problems, and even conflicts within our church body. Whether we stand or fall depends on the strength of our foundation. To do or not to do, that is the question.

A Centurion's Approach

Luke 7:1–10

Sometimes it's bewildering to try to sort out all the approaches to get the power of God working in our situation. It seems that new and different ways of getting God's power on our side are constantly being presented. Some teachers tell us that if we don't pray and act a certain way and follow certain procedures, God will not help us. Others say that God has much bigger things to do than bother with our little problems.

The centurion had obviously not been instructed in these ways. He simply sent word to Jesus concerning the desperate condition of his ill servant. This man recognized the authority of Jesus, and this realization brought him to a position of humility before the Master. He would not go personally to Jesus, for he was a gentile, a Roman officer sent by Caesar to occupy the land of the Jews. He sent word by those in a more appropriate position to approach Jesus.

This centurion understood authority, for he was a man under the authority of higher ranking officers. He was also an officer with many others under his command. His approach was to openly recognize Jesus' authority and ask that this divine power be released on behalf of his servant. Jesus was impressed and referred to the centurion's approach as that of great faith. The centurion realized that his own authority and personal power was inadequate. He also realized that he could not depend on the power of those over him and relied completely on the power and authority of Jesus.

Jesus said that all authority was given to Him under heaven and earth. He also said that without Him we can do nothing, but through Him all things are possible. Yet we approach Him as if He can do nothing without us and our programmed petition. I like the centurion's approach, humble recognition of the authority of Jesus and a simple request that He act in his behalf.

THE SOVEREIGN SAVIOR

LUKE 7:11–17

Much is said and taught about faith and healing. Many say that if you have enough faith, anything can and will be done. This is true if our faith is hinged to a word from God concerning his will in the matter. The only trouble is being sure of His will as our finite minds try to comprehend His wisdom and intellect, which are infinite. The Bible reminds us that His ways are not our ways. Who can know the mind of God? Who is man that God should consider him?

I would rather act in faith, thinking that I had a word from "His Word" and miss Him, than live and operate in a spiritually boring world of never believing God for anything. We must be careful not to fall into the trap of believing that the victory of Christian living depends on our faith rather than the sovereign power of God. God is all powerful and does a perfect job of doing whatever He wants to do. He wants us to call on Him and have faith in Him for that which He shows us to do, being mindful that He is sovereign and can do all things with or without our faith.

In considering the resurrection of the widow's son, we would have to say that the son had no faith, since he was dead. It does not seem likely that the mother expressed any faith, for she did not speak to Jesus. The Scripture says that he evaluated the situation, had compassion on those involved, and stopped the funeral by "speaking" the young man back to life. Jesus was free to demonstrate His love and compassion without anyone expressing any faith.

Jesus is our Sovereign Savior who is loving, compassionate and just. These characteristics will continue to be expressed by Him with or without our faith. However, it is wonderful to experience a special faith relationship with Him as we trust Him for everything in our daily walk. This can be experienced as we maintain a loving relationship with Him through regular, consistent prayer and study of the Scriptures. Prayer based on Scriptural principles is the springboard we must rely on to express and practice faith in our Sovereign God.

THE HEALING WORD

LUKE 7:18–23

We all get discouraged, depressed, and downhearted. Even the strongest, most mature Christians have their days of mixed emotions about their true position in Jesus. Their mind tells them all is well in spite of the circumstances, but their heart is not in it.

John the Baptist had reached this point. If anyone could know for sure who Jesus was, it would be John. Didn't he leap in his mother's womb when Mary came to tell her about the miraculous conception? Wasn't John brought up by parents who had firsthand, personal experience with Almighty God? Was he not told that he was a special child with a special purpose and plan for his life? Had he not been baptizing and preaching the message of "repentance" in preparation for the coming Messiah?

How could this man become depressed and doubt that which he knew in his mind was truth, that Jesus Christ was the Son of God, the promised Messiah? It was because his heart was not in it. It happens to all of us. John became so frustrated that he sent two of his disciples to Jesus to ask if He were the Christ or if they should look for another. Jesus did not send John a letter or words of persuasion, but simply demonstrated that which was written in the Word. Those disciples went back to John and told him what Jesus had done and immediately his heart was recommitted. The Word had come alive once again in his heart. His knowledge of the Old Testament became light unto his path, as the Scriptures were brought to life by the actions of Jesus. The Word became a healing for John's soul.

So it is with us. Jesus is faithful to bring the Word to life if we remain consistent in studying the Word and faithful in our fellowship with Him. We do well when we go to the Word and seek His face if we become discouraged, and our heart is not in it anymore.

GREATNESS IS GOING WITH GOD

LUKE 7:24–30

The world is full of people with great and glorious ideas. There are people everywhere with million-dollar dreams or the desire for great personal accomplishment in politics, music, or some other area. The problem is that few are single-minded enough to accomplish the things of which they dream. There are simply too many distractions. We give our time to many other areas which do not help us accomplish our dreams. Many times they even hinder the attaining of our goals.

Paul wrote, "...but this one thing I do..." How wonderful to see someone recognize their purpose in life and then press on to accomplish it. It is a beautiful thing to observe someone who has received their goal, their dream, their purpose from God and then devote their life to accomplishing it.

My life's goal has been to build a family, a family centered on God and His principles. My prayer is and has been that my children would come to know Jesus as personal Savior and Lord and then serve Him faithfully throughout their life. I claim this prayer not only for my children, but for their children, their children's children, and each successive generation until Jesus comes. A family established on The Rock, nurtured by the Word, and strengthened by the loving discipline of the Spirit of God through single-minded parents, is a worthy goal and a lifetime endeavor.

Jesus commended John the Baptist as the greatest born of woman, because he had one purpose assigned to him by God, and he remained faithful to it all his life. His task was simple: To prepare the way before Jesus as the promised messenger. This he did, in the face of much difficulty, and Jesus pronounced him great. Greatness is going with God.

I'd Rather Do It My Way

LUKE 7:31–35

There are many times along the path of life when we reject the advice and council of others and do it our own way. Sometimes this is the way to go if we have prayed, evaluated the circumstances, and received a word from God. But there are many times when we simply do it our way because of pride or rebellion against an authority.

Sometimes, we truly think we are correct in our human evaluation of the situation without seeking God's direction. We see this when a marriage ends in divorce without the effort of self-discipline or the advise of counsel to help make it work. We see this in job changes that come about over anger and resentment toward our boss or fellow workers. We even see this happen in good causes, like the battle for human rights, where an individual fighting for a good cause becomes so hostile over the circumstances that he becomes like those he is fighting against. The prevailing attitude seems to be, "If I don't like my situation, I'll rebel against it." This can be seen in the attitude of husbands, wives, children, employees, church members, pastors, and others toward their circumstances. Paul was engaged in the battle of rebellion against God's will for his life when Jesus spoke to him and said, "it is hard for thee to kick against the pricks." (Acts 9:56)

Jesus pointed out this flaw in humanity by showing the crowd that even though John the Baptist came fasting and drinking no wine (as a prophet), they rejected him as having a devil. This same crowd now rejected Jesus because He associated with sinners and publicans, eating and drinking with them. Jesus was saying that this was God's way, and it was being rejected with the haughty attitude of, "I'd rather do it my way."

Then Jesus spoke of wisdom, as if to say that those who have wisdom will act like it. The actions, attitudes, and reactions of those with wisdom will reflect wisdom. The Bible says that wisdom from above is pure, peaceable, and easy to be corrected or persuaded of that which is right. Wisdom, then, is the opposite of, "I'd rather do it my way." It is, in fact, an attitude of, "I must do it God's way."

48

SEARCHING, SEARCHING, AND NEVER SERVING

LUKE 7:36–50

It is such a delight to find a new word or a new truth or a new principle from God's Word! However, the search for these new truths can be a trap that keeps us from the greatest joy of the Christian life–a personal, loving relationship with Him. We sit in the pews taking notes, analyzing and comparing during the sermon. We attend the new Bible study; attend the Bible conference across town and in our own church. The Sunday Bible study becomes a time for historical delving into the Word.

This is all good, but if we become so wrapped up in this that we miss the joy of experiencing a flow of love between us and the Savior each day, we become cold and dry spiritually. If the new truth does not make us kneel at His feet and praise Him and love Him, we have missed the point. If it does not give us a deeper desire to serve Him by sharing the Gospel with others, we have missed the joy of a personal fellowship with Him. Searching, searching, never serving is a trap we must avoid.

The Pharisee invited Jesus so that He could analyze Him, study His behavior, and judge whether or not He was a true prophet. He was so preoccupied with this firsthand study of Jesus that he missed the wonderful privilege of washing His feet, anointing His head, and fellowshipping with the King of Kings. He was searching but not serving.

The woman, on the other hand, did just the opposite. She knew enough about Jesus and just wanted to love Him and worship Him. She knew that He loved sinners like her and that He would receive her love and praise. This overwhelmed her and she became caught up in her act of worship.

Jesus commended the actions of the woman and condemned those of the Pharisee who was searching without responding to the truth revealed.

NEVER GIVE UP!

LUKE 8:1–15

Have you ever shared the Word with someone as it related to salvation or to a defeated area of their life only to find that it was rejected? Have you ever felt God's blessing of liberty and clarity of explanation as you shared the Gospel with someone, only to see your witness rejected? Many of us have experienced this as we repeatedly shared with a friend or loved one who desperately needed the truth of salvation or the truth as it related to an area of need in their life. The tendency is to give up and say, "What's the use?" We must never do this. We must keep on praying for them, sharing with them, and living a victorious life before them. Never give up or become discouraged to the point of quitting. New people will cross the path of your life. Some will respond, while others will not. Never give up; never, never, never!

Jesus showed this truth in the parable of the sower. Some will reject the Word, some will receive it but not commit to it, some will receive it and grow with one foot in this world and one foot in the spiritual world, but some will receive the Word, commit their lives to Jesus, and grow to bear much fruit. Never give up!

Paul wrote, "I am made all things to all men, that I might by all means save some." He never gave up. Jesus taught us that as they rejected Him, so will they reject us. How can we hope to win everyone and see all the backslidden turn at our pleading, when many did not respond to Jesus?

Jesus taught us that people would not only reject us but would, at times, even persecute us. He also said that we were not to worry about what to say or what to do, because He would supply the words and the strength as the need arose. We must not become uptight or defeated when people reject our witness or the truth we share. After all, they do not reject us, but Jesus. He never gave up on people, and neither should we.

UNQUENCHABLE LIGHT

LUKE 8:16–18

Someone gave an illustration of the relationship between light and darkness that stuck with me over the years. If we are in a lighted room on a dark night and open the door, the darkness will not flood the lighted room, but rather the light will push the darkness away. The light cannot be contained. It seems to leak out under the door, through creases in the curtains and even up the chimney.

So it is with the Christian life. If Christ is in us and is in charge of our walk, His light will shine through us. It will flood the darkness of wrong attitudes, hostile meetings, and hopeless situations. This light is going to naturally (or actually supernaturally) shine unless it is hindered. It can be put under the vessel of fear about what others will think or say, or the vessel of ignorance of the Word which hinders the Holy Spirit from responding through us to these dark situations, or the vessel of failure to pray and have a quiet time with the Lord every day. The truth is that this light wants to shine; it is built to shine, and the only way it will fail to shine is because of deliberate hindrance by us.

This same truth applies to the influence of the life without God. The light of a life that goes its own way, pursuing the things of the world, will shine and touch lives all about it. The light of movie stars, athletes, beauty queens, political and business leaders reaches out to deeply influence the lives of thousands with which it comes in contact. The problem is that many times, this is a false light. It is actually darkness dressed up like light, but this light is not unquenchable.

The light of Jesus and the life controlled by Him and the Word will displace the false light. This new light in Him is unquenchable except it be put under a vessel of hindrance. Let your light shine; it can only be hindered by you.

PART OF THE FAMILY

LUKE 8:19–21

Belonging to the family has long been a cherished lifestyle for many of us. I still look forward to our family reunion each year. To recall the endearing times we had together as children and young adults brings an inner joy that can hardly be explained. These are wonderful, priceless possessions which required great sacrifices of love, patience and understanding by those who went before us as part of the family.

There is a greater family relationship that lasts forever. We become a part of this family by committing our life to Jesus Christ in faith. We grow as a part of this family when we experience the deep personal relationships with Jesus as we pass through the times of joy and testing. We establish relationships with other members of the family, and again endearing times are logged. The opportunity to be a part of this family also requires great sacrifices of love, mercy and grace. These family relationships would not be possible except for Jesus Christ who paid the penalty for our sins by His death on the cross and by His resurrection from the grave to share the power of victory in this life with us.

When Jesus was told that His earthly family was waiting to see Him, He said that all were His family who heard the Word of God and did what it said. The Word of God says that all have sinned and fallen short of the worthiness to be a part of His family. The Word of God also says that those who receive Him are given the power to become the children of God. To receive Jesus as Savior and Lord makes us a part of the family of God forever. It also makes us brother and sister to the entire family.

How wonderful is the love and grace of our Lord that makes it possible for us to become a part of the family! Are you a part of the family? You can become a member of God's family now by asking Him to forgive your sins and receive Jesus as Savior.

JESUS' CLASSROOM

LUKE 8:22–25

One of the most dramatic stories I have ever heard is the one about the man who had a drinking problem and went out every week to return late at night drunk. His wife fretted and prayed over this for years until one evening the man once again started out to his watering hole. It was cold, and a light snow was on the ground. The man stopped a short distance from his home, and looking back saw his young son following behind. He noticed that the little boy was stretching to place his small feet in the tracks left by his dad. The man scolded the boy and asked what he thought he was doing, and the young son looked wide-eyed up at his father and said, "I am following in your footprints, Daddy."

Jesus used His daily footprints to lead and teach his followers lasting truth. In this account, Jesus had already said that they were going to the other side of the lake. When the storm came and Jesus was sleeping, the disciples became so caught up in the circumstances of the moment that they forgot what Jesus said. After they woke Him, He calmed the storm and then asked where their faith was. He was saying, "Class is open, men. Did I not say we were going to the other side? Was I not calm and even sleeping? Then why should you get uptight over circumstances after I have given you a word about the outcome?"

His class is also in session everyday for us. What is He trying to teach us through the circumstances of today? Have we become distracted in the classroom by the fears of tomorrow? Are we so preoccupied by our personal ambitions that we have missed His word about what our purpose and goals should be?

Our class is in session everyday also. What do people read from our footprints? What do we communicate by our actions and reactions? Where will our sons and daughters end up if they walk in our footprints? Class is always in session. What is the lesson for today?

WITH GOD, ALL THINGS ARE POSSIBLE

LUKE 8:26–36

Many are the times when we see our situation or the situation of another as impossible. Too often we see the circumstances of the entire world or the circumstances of our own little world as impossible. The Bible teaches that all circumstances work together for our benefit in the long run if we belong to Jesus. Somehow we don't see God as being in control when we can't understand the outcome of the situation. Nevertheless, He is in control. He is sovereign, and through Him all things are possible.

The account of the Gadarene demoniac is a great example of Jesus' ability to do anything and of His authority over everything on earth and in heaven. The man was possessed with demons, he went around naked, he lived in a cemetery and he was all alone, for no one wanted to be near him. His situation was impossible. The purpose of the demons was to destroy him, and this is still their purpose today. Art Linkletter could testify to that. His daughter got into drugs and leaped from a building to her death. There are many documented cases of famous people involved with drugs who ended with violent destruction. There must be thousands of similar cases involving ordinary people that only made the local news. There are cases of destruction and death related to alcohol every day, and many believe that alcohol and drugs open the doors of our mind for demonic activity.

The good news is that Jesus had power over this seemingly impossible situation and still does today. The demons feared Him and recognized Him then as they do now. They are smarter than many of us. We rejected Him for years and refused to recognize Him as the Son of God, the Savior, yet these demons recognized Him and spoke to Him by name. We have an opportunity that they don't. We can receive Him as Savior and Lord of our lives. The man was healed from Gadara and sat at the feet of Jesus. He must have said, "With God all things are possible." So should we.

Greater Things Shall You Do

Luke 8:37–40

Have you ever thought, "If Jesus would just come to our town or our church, perform a miracle and then preach one of His great sermons, all these folks would receive Him as their Savior?" The truth of the matter is that He called every Christian to be a witness for Him. We are charged with the responsibility and privilege of sharing Christ with the world we live in by sharing what He has done and is doing for us personally. We are to show in word and by our lifestyle that Christ can do, and wants to do, great things for all who will receive him.

Jesus provided us with the power to do what He charged us to do - be His witnesses. He even told His disciples (and us) that we would do greater things than He did. Why not? We have the Word, the Holy Spirit living in us, and we have the personal experience of our salvation. He has equipped us to do greater things than He did - it is His will and desire for our lives. "You shall receive power after that the Holy Ghost is come upon you and you shall be my witnesses both in Jerusalem and Judea and Samaria and the uttermost parts of the Earth" (Acts 1:8).

The healed Gadarene wanted to go with Jesus but was instructed to go back to the place where he lived and worked and be a witness as to what Jesus had done for him. We have the same tendency as the Gadarene. When we are saved, get into the Word, and experience the joy of worshipping the Lord, we'd rather just stay there but we too must go and tell others what great things He has done for us.

The strange truth in this account is that the people of the country asked Jesus to leave. They did not want to hear Him or have Him around, but they did hear the healed one and see the change in his life. Then when Jesus came back, they received Him gladly. They did not receive Jesus until they saw the one healed by Him. "Greater things than this shall you do."

THE NEED OF THE RELIGIOUS

LUKE 8:41–42, 49–56

Jairus was a ruler of the Synagogue which means that he was in responsible charge of the religious services and the order of things at the church house of that day. This also means that he was a part of a long family line that inherited this job all the way down through the Levites, beginning with Aaron in the days of Moses. He was a religious man, but he had a need. He had come to the end of his self-sufficiency for his only daughter was dying, and he was desperate.

Jesus overheard the words of hopelessness delivered to Jairus, "Thy daughter is dead; trouble not the Master." In other words, the crisis is over so you don't need Jesus anymore. Jesus responded with words of hope and the admonition to believe.

Jairus must have responded in belief for they went to the house even though the girl had been pronounced dead. The friends and family laughed at Jesus when he told them not to cry for the girl was only asleep. In so doing, they also belittled Jairus since he had invited Jesus to come even after he received word that she was dead. Ignoring their ridicule, Jesus raised the girl from the dead, and her parents were astonished.

Many of us fall in the category of religious folks who need Jesus. We may come from a family line of Christians who have belonged to this or that denomination. We may seek personal relationships with Jesus only when we are desperate. We are plagued with that old saying, "God helps those who help themselves" or "God gave us a brain and He doesn't expect us to bother Him with this or that." The truth is, we all need a close relationship with Jesus day by day in every situation of life. The Bible says that we are to be careful for nothing, but to make our wishes known to Him with prayer and thanksgiving. He is waiting to show Himself strong on our behalf, and we desperately need His input in every one of life's situations.

JESUS FIRST

LUKE 8:43–48

I have talked to parents whose children have been on drugs or alcohol, and almost without exception they never suspected. They are always the last to know. The call from the police station is usually their first knowledge of the fact that there is a problem. Why is it when we are in trouble, the last ones we confide in are the ones who love us most? Maybe we don't want to hurt them, but they usually find out anyway and the hurt is deepened.

Too often we do the same thing with Jesus. We try it on our own; we spend hours and days trying to work it out; we confide in everyone but Jesus. Why do we wait until last to confide in Jesus, when He knows it anyway?

The woman in the scriptures had tried everything. She had exhausted her resources, and finally, as a last resort, she sought out Jesus and touched Him. If she had just gone to Him first! But then what about us? If we had just gone to Him first.

Somehow we look on those who trust Jesus as Savior and Lord early in their life as not having an exciting salvation experience. The truth of the matter is that they have an early start with Him; they have not established bad habits and lifestyles that are hard to change; they have not wasted years of service and fellowship opportunities with Him and with His family.

Note that Jesus felt the virtue leave as the woman touched Him. This indicated that the price for healing was already paid and just stored up in Him waiting to be released. The price for our salvation, our personal relationship with Him, our ability to understand the scripture and walk in victory is already paid. He is just waiting, calling, and inviting us to receive it in faith. Why not Jesus first?

COMMISSION BY CHRIST

LUKE 9:1–6

In days of old, a person sent out by the reigning monarch had the authority to accomplish his mission in the power of the king who sent him. To cross this ambassador or do him harm was as if the king who sent him was rebuked, and it usually meant war, unless satisfactory restitution was made. This principle still applies today between nations.

Jesus commissioned the twelve and gave them a power and authority to heal and to cast out devils. This is a power they did not have before or Jesus would not need to give it to them. Jesus was very specific in his instructions, and the disciples went in power. They accomplished that which He told them to do. They went in His authority and in His power to do that which He told them to do.

Many times we fail in our efforts for Jesus because we are not moving on His orders. We move on impulse or emotion, because someone else is doing it, or because someone else got a word from God. We must not be intimidated by what God sends someone else to do. To know His will for us, we must be in the Word, in prayer, in regular corporate worship and sensitive to the leading of the Holy Spirit. Notice that the disciples were close enough to Him that they heard His call: "He called them," gave them instruction, and they went out on His orders and in His authority.

When Jesus calls us and gives us instructions to do something, we are given His power and authority to accomplish that which He calls us to do. Arthur Blessit pulled a cross all over the world as God directed. It seems foolish, but it works for him because he was doing what God told him to do. The Sunday school teacher or outreach leader who is acting on God's Word is successful in His power and authority because he was commissioned by Christ. When we fail, it is not necessarily because we have not been commissioned by Him but because we have not claimed all the power and authority available to us.

THE PERPLEXED SEEKER

LUKE 9:7–9

The Scripture says that Herod was perplexed, and well he should have been. Rumors were reaching him everyday concerning Jesus. Some were saying that Elijah had appeared, and others were saying that one of the prophets of long past has risen from the dead. These rumors probably did not bother Herod, but the one that reported Jesus as being John the Baptist was perplexing. Herod had killed John because he spoke out against the sins in his life, and the prospect of this one coming back from the grave must have been frightening. Herod reasoned that if he could just see this one called Jesus, it would all be settled, so he became a perplexed seeker.

This sequence of events in Herod's life is similar in many ways to what we experience today. Who among us has not rejected the Word? Have we not refused to read and study the Scriptures to see what God has for us? Have we not read or heard the Word and rejected it thereby killing the effectiveness of the prophets of old? As we refuse to read the Scriptures and study them on a regular basis or as we reject the Word which we read or hear, we become self-sufficient, rejecting the Christ of whom the Scriptures speak.

Then a difficult or frightening situation comes, and we become perplexed. Have we ever attempted to bargain with God by resolving to "look into" this matter of Christianity? We look for a way to keep on doing what we are doing without getting too deeply involved with Jesus. We really seek not to find Him but to justify our actions. We become perplexed seekers. We need to be broken seekers, willing to admit our wrong and willing to receive Jesus as the Lord and Savior He is. We must be broken, repenting Christians when we find ourselves out of His will, eager to get back into fellowship with Him.

THE LORD'S PROVISION

LUKE 9:10–17

It seems we never have enough time. We seem to always be in a hurry, and the beauty of the day streaks by without our notice. I catch myself competing as I drive to work, or I find myself irritated with someone who pulls over in the space I have grudgingly left between me and the car in front. If we could learn to glance about in our hurry and pray for those all about us, I think we would reap a new dimension of His blessing.

The lady speeding by may have left a home in shambles, her children may be sick, her husband may be leaving her, or any number of hurts could be troubling her. We have the opportunity to ask God to help us pray on her behalf. The same could be said of all those who flash by as we speed on our way.

We even miss the opportunity to thank God and praise Him for the beauty of His creation. "Thou art worthy, oh Lord, to receive glory and honor and power: for thou hast created all things and for thy pleasure they are and were created" (Rev. 4:11).

Jesus gives us a good example in this scripture. He went aside as if to hide from the multitude so that He could be alone with his apostles. Somehow the people found out and when they showed up, He received them. For the most part we do not receive people unless it is convenient. In fact, we get rather put out sometimes when they seek help in the midst of our busy schedule.

Jesus not only received them but He ministered to their needs. Is it possible that we do not minister unless it is planned and prearranged? The Lord's provision was all they needed. Those that needed healing were healed, and all that were hungry had opportunities to eat. Jesus had just sent the disciples out with the power to accomplish a mission. Now he was demonstrating the act of ministering on the spot in the "Lord's provision." Lord, help us to be sensitive to the opportunities you put before us each day to minister in your provisions.

WHAT DO YOU SAY?

LUKE 9:18–22

An old form of greeting still used in some areas today is, "What do you say?" Another way of putting it is, "What's the good word?" or "How are you today?" These are friendly greetings.

There is a more important question; in fact, it is one of the most important questions in life. The question is, "What do you say about Christ?" The most important question in life is what have you done with Christ personally, but this can only be answered after we have settled the question of what do we say about Him. What do you say about Christ?

Jesus asked the question point blank, "Whom do the people say that I am?" His disciples responded by telling him that the people were saying that He was John the Baptist, Elijah, or one of the other prophets risen from the dead. Then Jesus got to the most important issue, that is, "Whom do you say that I am?" To this, Peter responded, "You are the Christ of God." God had shown Peter that Jesus was the promised Messiah, the Savior, the Lord and the Redeemer spoken of in the Old Testament.

Peter was far from being all Jesus wanted him to be, but this was a basic fundamental beginning along the road that would lead him to become what Jesus wanted him to be. As the life, death, resurrection, and ascension of Jesus unfolded before Peter and as he experienced the love, grace, and mercy of Jesus, he became a stronghold for the Faith.

Jesus knew what the people were saying about Him. He also knew what Peter would say about Him, but he must have wanted to hear Peter say it. There's something firm and final about saying it.

What do you say about Jesus? Is He just a prophet of old, a good man, or a foolish man who claimed to be the Son of God? He is the Son of God, the Lord and Savior, whether you say it or not. Receive this truth so that you can then receive Him as your personal Savior. Commit yourself to Him as Lord of your life so that you can start becoming what He wants you to be. Only He knows what you could be, and only you can let it happen.

The Cost Of Discipleship

Luke 9:23–27

Thomas Edison gave himself to the invention of the electric light bulb. He worked day and night with all his strength and concentration toward this end. He gave himself completely to the task, and everything about him became a part of this effort. It cost him many comforts and indulgences, but it paid off and his name is synonymous with the invention of the electric light bulb. Although it cost him much, it paid him more in satisfaction, the feeling of accomplishment, and financial gain. There are many other accounts of men and women who gave themselves totally to a task or dream.

Jesus warned His disciples that the cost of following Him was total commitment. The things of the world were not to be a distraction from God's purpose for their lives. Instead, worldly activities were to be focused on as opportunities to minister in their commitments to serve, love, and praise God in every aspect of life.

Jesus seemed to warn them that the main deterrent would be the quest for material gain. "What shall a man advantage if he gains the whole world and lose himself, or be a castaway?" Jesus also seemed to say that the pursuit of material gain as our main objective would conflict with our commitment to Him to the point that we would become ashamed of Him.

These truths hold for us today. We must commit to His lordship as Edison committed to the invention of the light bulb. Everything about us must blend into this commitment. Our work, our family, our church and even our victories and defeats should be in harmony with discipleship. Anything that causes us to be ashamed of Him is out of place and a distraction to the main objective. Discipleship costs, but it also pays with the joy and peace which comes through fellowship with Him in all things.

WHEN WE SEE JESUS

LUKE 9:28–36

Do you know what Jesus looks like? There are no photographs of Him. There are no paintings of Him that were done during His lifetime on earth. There are no detailed descriptions of Him except a brief one by Isaiah which was spoken hundreds of years before His birth. Will we know Him when we see him face to face?

Jesus took Peter and John up on a mountain to pray. While they were there, Jesus took on a different appearance, and Moses and Elijah appeared with Him. The Scriptures do not say how Peter and John knew these two men were Moses and Elijah. Clearly, they did not introduce themselves. Instead, it appears that they completely ignored Peter and John, concentrating on Jesus. It seems to me that everybody just automatically knew each other. Although Jesus appeared somehow different ("His countenance was altered"), the two apostles recognized Him. Moses and Elijah had never met Jesus face to face (except perhaps in the "burning bush" experience of Moses or the "storm" experience of Elijah), but they knew Him, and Jesus and the apostles knew them.

I will not worry about knowing Jesus when I see Him face to face, for I'll recognize Him immediately and instinctively. I think that I shall recognize everyone in heaven the same way, even ancestors who had a part in shaping my life and who had gone on before my time. I won't need an old photograph to recognize my mother or father or thousands of others that I need to recognize to the glory and honor of Jesus.

God the Father only spoke concerning His Son. The others were not that important. When we see Jesus, everything and everybody will fade into the background, and He will be first, foremost, and preeminent. Oh, God, hasten the day when we see Jesus in His glory.

DOWN FROM THE MOUNTAIN

LUKE 9:37–42

We can all remember those mountain-top experiences when God seemed to speak to us alone and showed us a great victory through His power and grace. There are times when everything seems to be on track, and our lives are meshed with the Lord in such a way that the fellowship and communion with Him is so real. Then we are faced with the suffering and lostness about us. If we were allowed to remain on the mountain-top, we would grow cold toward those in darkness without Christ. We would look past those of the family who suffer and are going through a dark time in their lives. The mountain-tops are great, but they are designed to give us momentum as we come down to minister and share Christ in the valley.

Jesus, Peter, and John had just been on the mountain where Moses and Elijah had appeared, and where God the Father had spoken. Peter was so moved that he wanted to stay on the mountain and build a memorial to the occasion. God's instructions were to "Hear His Son," and His Son Jesus said, "Follow Me." I think this means read My Word, watch what I do, see the revelations and instructions for your life as I share the experiences of My life here on Earth with you. Let Me live in you and project My love, peace and joy through you.

Jesus demonstrated the lifestyle in the valley as the man came to Him concerning his son who was taken by a spirit of the devil. Jesus had just had a mountain-top experience with the Father, but immediately following, He ministered to the needs of a desperate father and his only child. It seems that the close intimate times with the Father are always followed by someone seeking us out for help. We must be ready, as Jesus was, to come down from the mountain sensitive to those needs that are laid out before us in the valley.

RESERVE POWER

LUKE 9:43–45

Most automobiles are equipped with a passing gear so that a reserve power is available when it is needed. The carburetors on many of these cars have a "secondary" that allows more fuel to surge into the combustion chamber so that a reserve power is available in an emergency situation. Doctors tell us that there is a reserve power in our bodies that gives us unbelievable strength in a panic situation. There are accounts of people lifting large, heavy objects off someone, but when they went back to lift that object again, it was physically impossible.

We also need a reserve power spiritually. When the trials of life come we must be able to call on a supernatural, spiritual strength that is deep within us. When the death of a loved one is at hand, when the finances that are necessary for the support of our family fail, when we are rejected by those we love most, or when those we love most do not respond to the Gospel, we need a reserve, spiritual power.

Jesus had been on the mountain with Peter and John when they witnessed the unbelievable "transfiguration experience." They had seen Him perform many unbelievable miracles and even experienced the power and authority He gave them as they went out under His instructions. Now they had seen Him cast out an unclean spirit with which they were unable to deal.

Then Jesus gave them instructions which they did not understand. He simply said, "Let these sayings sink down into your ears, "for the Son of Man shall be delivered into the hands of men." He was telling them that they would need to draw on those things they had seen and heard from Him. He was showing them that when all looked hopeless and dark they would need this reserve power—and so will we. We must feed on the Word every day and constantly recall His faithfulness in times past. We must consistently talk to Him in a personal, intimate prayer life in order to have that reserve power.

BIG IS LITTLE

LUKE 9:46–50

Have you ever noticed that little children compete to determine who will be the leader? Sometimes they change the games they play, not so much because they like the new game better, but that a change of leadership will occur and place another at the top. This quest for power must be innate. We do not have to teach it to our children. Even adults vie for positions of leadership.

It is also notable that those who don't make it to the top seem to be well equipped with criticism of those who reach positions of leadership. Even those who appear to be born followers seem to have a complex about not being leaders, for we frequently hear weak and fragile excuses as to why they don't want the leadership role.

Jesus' disciples reasoned among themselves who should be the greatest. From this Jesus taught a great truth that reaches down into the spiritual depth of our lives. Jesus was teaching that humility is the key to being great for God and that the new nature of the saved person, with the indwelling Spirit, would supernaturally have the same Spirit as Jesus. The Scriptures say that Jesus "thought it not robbery to be equal with God; but made himself of no reputation," and humbled Himself. We must humble ourselves as the Holy Spirit nudges our spirit, thereby having the same mind in us that was in Jesus.

One of the surest tests that checks out our position of humility is how we view those that are not "like us" - those that are not of "our group" or of "our denomination." Jesus rebuked the disciples for judging those who were not followers of their group although they cast out devils in Jesus' name. So shall He rebuke us when we get too big for our spiritual britches. To be big by God's measure is to assume our proper size alongside Him.

THE PRINCE OF PATIENCE

LUKE 9:51–56

When I first started sharing my faith, I was very relieved when it was over. I often became dismayed or frustrated when someone would not respond favorably to Christ. Finally I progressed to the point of fully realizing that Jesus died for those to whom I was sharing the good news as well as for me. If He didn't give up and become irritated with them, then why should I? This developing revelation gives me peace and security as I share my life and the Gospel with those God puts me in contact with during my normal, everyday life situations.

Why should I become frustrated and irritated because they do not respond immediately? Did not Jesus have to work with me over a long period of time? He is the Prince of Patience, and He will come to that person another day through another witness or circumstance. We must continue to show the light of the Gospel in our lifestyle and pray for those we witness to until Jesus Himself releases us. Someone has said that as faithful witnesses we are to share the Gospel and leave the results to God.

The disciples became frustrated and irritated when the village rejected Jesus. Their response was to see if Jesus wanted the entire village to be destroyed by fire. But the patient, loving, forgiving Prince of Peace showed them that they had missed the point. In fact, He went so far as to point out that this reaction came from "another spirit." Jesus in effect said that He had come to save people not destroy them.

They departed with a strong implication that somehow these people would be given another chance. How many shared with that one before we came along and reaped the harvest? We can be sure that the Prince of Patience was there before you or I came along.

IS THE LORD OUR LORD?

LUKE 9:57–62

There are many people who, as a youth or a young adult, had goals, plans, and good intentions to fulfill a special lifetime dream. The sad part is that later we find these same people on a different course, having long since given up their dream. This is because, in most cases, they let other things or projects get in the way. The dream became secondary and eventually faded into a memory.

The characters in this account of Luke all called Jesus "Lord", but they each had a more important obligation or task than following Him. They all meant well and were not ashamed to call Him Lord. The problem was that "the Lord" was not really "their lord." Jesus spoke of total commitment when He referred to ploughing while looking back. Every farm boy knows that you can't plough a straight row when you look back to see where you have already ploughed.

We are faced with the same temptation as Jesus calls us to let Him be Lord of our lives. As we get into the Word, pray and fellowship with Him, He usually bids us to follow Him in a special area. The call might be to be more faithful to Him through our church, to be a better parent or husband or wife, to teach, to witness, to preach, or anyone of a thousand things He calls people to do.

How often we, like the characters in this account, say, "Lord, first I must do this thing or that thing before I can give myself to this calling." We call Him "Lord" but we give ourselves to other things and the most important opportunity of our life fades—to be His friend and follower fades away. Is the Lord really our Lord? Do we place Him first in our activities and commitments or do other things consistently take priority? Let us commit to make the Lord our Lord.

LABORING IN THE LORD'S HARVEST

LUKE 10:1–16

It is interesting to check the response on the other end of the telephone when we have the authority to use a certain person's name as a reference in our request to speak to someone. The name of a friend or a person with power will open the door for us, especially if we are going on their behalf. The opportunity to speak to that person is not because of our power, but because of the power and influence of the one who sent us.

This scripture speaks of the Lord of the harvest and His authority to send forth laborers. When we go out to witness, to share the good news of Jesus, to comfort and pray with a hurting friend or neighbor, we are laboring for the Lord of the harvest. We become His special force being "sent forth into His harvest." We do not go in our strength, but in His.

Jesus' instructions were simple. Humbly accept the hospitality that is offered and "fit in" with the atmosphere at the place of visitation. It is not our responsibility to make the people we visit receptive. That is the task of our Lord, for this is His harvest. We are to be careful that rejection is not caused by our attitude or behavior. In other words, we must be careful not to act in such a way as to squelch the Spirit who preceded us. He makes ready. We simply go expecting His presence.

In the event that rejection does result, we are to go on to another and leave the judgment to Jesus, the Lord of the harvest. If I call on a businessman in the name of his friend, he receives or rejects his friend as he receives or rejects me. The Bible speaks of us as ambassadors. Ambassadors are people who represent the authority of one nation to the authority of another nation. The old song says, "This is not my home, I'm just passing through"—I'm laboring for the Lord of the harvest.

PRIORITY IN PRAISE

LUKE 10:17–20

We are preoccupied with the unusual and the unknown. We seek after new worlds to explore, new heights to reach, and new discoveries to be made. This produces good things and good feelings, but many times we overlook the most important things in our search for the new and different. The gold miner digs into the side of the mountain looking for that rare nugget, while the artist places the beauty of the same mountain on canvas.

When we find a new word from God's Word, we get excited, and we should. When our spirit seems to flow with the Word of God and the Holy Spirit, we praise Him, and we should. However, we must never lose sight of the most important thing in life, the wonderful gift of salvation by God's Grace on the Cross. There must be priority in our praise and rejoicing.

Jesus pointed this out to the seventy disciples as they returned from the mission on which He had sent them. They marveled at the fact that "the devils are subject unto us through Thy Name" and Jesus responded by pointing out that He was present when satan was cast out of heaven.

I believe Jesus was saying that it is normal and natural for devils to be overpowered by the name of Jesus Christ, since it is by His power that they were cast out of heaven. Then Jesus reminded them that this power was given to them to accomplish the mission on which they were sent. It was not given so that they could "show off" this power, but so that He would be revealed to unbelieving hearts.

However, Jesus said, "Rejoice not in this but rather rejoice in that your names are written in heaven." Prioritize your praise, He seemed to say. Don't become caught up in what you can do in My Name, but rejoice because of who you are in My Name. As the chorus says, "Rejoice in the Lord always, and again I say rejoice."

REJOICING IN THE SPIRIT

LUKE 10:21–24

There are times when I recall something that my father said or did when I was young. I now began to see wisdom that I did not recognize at the time. It is almost as if he were teaching me through his actions or the statement of a principle that I could not or would not receive at the time. There are even times when I review some of his "old-fashioned" ideas with the conclusion that they were rather wise and appropriate. I consider this "teaching with a delayed fuse," for my dad has long since gone to be with the Lord. Nevertheless, his teaching lingers on to my joy, excitement, and benefit.

Jesus rejoiced in the Spirit over the truth that the greatest thing that can happen to a human being is to be saved. The perfect love, justice and consistency of God's plan for salvation stirred the heart of Jesus. Anyone may come, but all must come exactly the same way, as a little child or "babe." The rich, the poor, the "wise and prudent" as well as the simple minded may come, but they all must come humbly and simply.

To say that I'm wrong, I blew it, I am a sinner before a holy sovereign God and I confess I need help is the only route to salvation. To trust and receive Jesus as the only hope of salvation and eternal life is the way to life. The revelation of this truth does not come from our own intelligence, but from Jesus the Lord as He reveals it to us. This should make us rejoice in the Spirit with our Lord.

Like the disciples, Jesus also says to us, "Many prophets and kings have desired to see" this truth "and to hear" these things and have not. Great and godly men and women of Bible times looked forward and longed to see the revelations of Jesus the Christ. We live in the day after the fact of His birth, life on earth, death on the cross, bodily resurrection and ascension. Let us rejoice in the Spirit and resolve anew to share this greatest of all treasures with others.

NEIGHBORS ARE MORE THAN
THE PEOPLE NEXT DOOR

LUKE 10:25–37

All our lives we hear or speak of our next-door neighbor, and every time we hear or read this parable of the "Good Samaritan" we naturally think of our next-door neighbor. As a child I was raised on a farm in East Texas, where our nearest neighbor was about a mile away. In West Texas some people have to go many miles to get to their nearest neighbor. Neighbors are not necessarily next door.

The lawyer who questioned Jesus about who his neighbor was represents many of us who legalistically try to limit the obligation of this great commandment, "Love thy neighbor as thyself." The lawyer wanted to get to heaven, but he didn't want to receive this commandment as encompassing too many people along the way.

I believe Jesus' answer to the question, "Who is my neighbor?" includes every person with whom we come in contact who has a need that we can meet. They all need prayer. We can take a moment to offer up a prayer to God on their behalf. Some need physical help. We can help them find that through our church or our own personal involvement. Most of them just need someone to show that they care and are truly interested.

Notice that the Samaritan neither did not stay with the man but went his way after ministering to his immediate needs and making provision for his future needs. True compassion does not mean moving in with someone, but it does mean getting our lives involved with theirs.

Our best approach to this question is to simply do what the lawyer did. Ask Jesus to show us who our neighbor is. If we listen, we will find, as the lawyer did, that our neighbor is more than the people next door.

MINISTERING AS YOU GO

LUKE 10:38–42

When I attended Texas A&M University we had a "religious emphasis week" once each year. A preacher or an evangelist would come and preach an hour each day for a week. In our church we have an emphasis on witnessing or a Bible conference or a revival meeting which lasts for a week or more. Then we settle back to life as usual, thinking many times, "Thank goodness that's over." The truth is that the Bible teaches that we should minister as we go, witness as we go, share as we go, and pray and study the Bible as we go. Jesus demonstrated this principle in His own life here on Earth.

This account says, "as they went, he entered into a certain village, and a certain woman named Martha received Him into her house." Jesus used this time to fellowship and teach truth about real-life situations. He ministered as He went, being very sensitive to the deeper needs of those with whom He came in contact. Jesus did not really rebuke Martha for being troubled and careful about many things but simply reminded her that she needed one thing more—to listen to the words of the Lord as He spoke. The food Martha prepared and the setting for the table would soon be gone, but the teachings of Jesus would be food for her soul forever.

The main point is that Jesus ministered as He went. He received invitations to people's homes. He shared on the street. He invited Himself into the homes of some people. He used storms and fig trees and the weather to show spiritual principles relative to living situations. We must do the same. How can we keep from ministering as we go when we have the same living Christ abiding in us? We must be sensitive to those gentle inner nudges that alert us to a ministry opportunity.

LEARN AND DO

LUKE 11:1–13

Many times I have sought to learn how to do something only to lose the desire or the skill over the years to come. I worked very hard to learn how to play golf many years ago, but I lost interest and have not played in years. I could hardly wait to get an old antique car to rebuild and tinker with. This I did and worked with it for years, but the desire and discipline to continue faded, and the old car sits in the garage covered with quilts and blankets.

The disciples saw Jesus pray and asked Him to teach them to pray. He quickly and simply told them how to pray, but the greater part of His response was not on how to pray but on the consistency of prayer. He also emphasized the fact that the Father wants us to pray and desires to give us good things in response to our prayers. The Bible says that we are to pray without ceasing, that we have not because we ask not and that we are to pray with hearts and words of praise and thanksgiving.

I feel that we know how to pray well enough. The problem is that we do not discipline ourselves in consistent prayer. The Spirit is standing by to prompt us and help us pray. The Bible is there to give us thoughts, words and principles in which our prayers are rooted. The Bible teaches that we do not know how to pray as we should but the Holy Spirit helps. We simply need to practice prayer by talking to God honestly and gladly.

We learn by instruction and teaching, but we perfect a skill by doing it. Learn from the Master how to pray and continue with Him under the tutelage of the Holy Spirit toward perfect prayer. Learn to pray - then do it, and keep on doing it.

A STRONG FRIEND

LUKE 11:14–26

Every child experiences the bully syndrome. There is always one that seems destined to pick on us and shove us around when we are in grade school. Then there seems to come that day when someone bigger than the bully takes a liking to us. At last there comes the confrontation of our strong friend and the bully at which time we are liberated. The only problem is that if this is a passing relationship or a moment of compassion on the part of our liberator, the bully comes again with even more intimidation. I had a friend like this who became a true friend. He was a little older than me, but he really liked me and we had fun together. He seemed to always be near, and I had no problems with bullies. He was a strong friend.

Jesus gives an account of casting out an evil spirit in which He emphasizes the fact that the strong also prevail in the spiritual world. He makes it clear that all power to deal with the devil and his forces is His. He also makes it clear that if the evil spirits return and find no resistance, they will take over with greater intensity than before. However, if Jesus remains, the evil one cannot come back in a greater force or on a permanent basis. If Jesus is allowed to move in and have control when the evil spirit leaves, how can the evil spirit re-occupy? Jesus becomes the strong friend who expels the bully and who is always around to keep him in his place.

Jesus said that He who is within us is greater than he who is in the world. Jesus said that it was better for Him to go so that the Holy Spirit could come and be in us and for us. When we have Jesus as Savior and Lord we have a strong, permanent friend. He is also a gentleman and will not bully His way into our lives. He comes in only by invitation. Ask Him in today if you have not already done so.

EACH IS ACCOUNTABLE

LUKE 11:27–28

I have always admired people of the Bible who received a word from God and acted on it in the power and provisions of Him who spoke it. I have been, and am being, strengthened and encouraged by individuals of today who live and operate on the basis of God's Word and the power of the indwelling Christ. However, these great disciples of yesterday and today will not make my life Christ-centered or Christ-filled. I must act on my own to study the Word, actively participate in worship, submit myself to the preaching and teaching of God's Word, pray consistently, and respond to the constant fellowship of my Lord as He directs my life.

An unnamed woman is quoted in this scripture to show this truth. She saw the powerful, loving and compassionate life of Jesus and thought of His mother. How wonderful to have been the mother of Jesus! As we recall the beautiful submission of Mary to the call of God, we are thrilled and encouraged. So must this woman have been as she spoke words of admiration for Mary. Then Jesus brought her back to reality by reminding her that it is more important for each of us to respond, like Mary, to the direction of God in her life. Our admiration for a committed believer will not substitute for our personal commitment.

Each is accountable. Though we may be encouraged by the powerful life of another, it is our personal response to God each day in every situation that really counts. These responses are directly related to our understanding of the Word and our personal relationship to Jesus.

"No one cometh to the Father but by me, "Jesus said. He also said that without Him we could do nothing. "Why do you call me Lord, and do not the things that I say?" He also promised the guiding presence of the indwelling Holy Spirit to those who receive Him as Savior and Lord. Each is accountable.

BEWARE OF SIGNS

LUKE 11:29–36

Many times when I become frustrated over a decision that needs to be made or an action that needs to be taken, I am tempted to proposition God for a sign. This may be a proper action if I have been in His Word consistently, praying for insight and wisdom continually and evaluating circumstances cautiously. Circumstances are controlled by factors other than God as He permits them to happen. God's priorities for altering circumstances may place my request for a sign in a position far below the needs of others. To allow a sign in response to my request may be considered by someone else as a sign that would be contrary to God's will for their life. I recall someone pointing out that for God to answer his prayer and bless a certain stock, a vast increase in financial gain would occur for many who were in rebellion against God's will for their lives.

Jesus pointed out several things in this scripture. He reminded these people that He, the Son of God, had come to preach the good news and was being rejected, while Jonah had gone to a heathen city where the people listened and repented. He said that a queen came a long way to hear the words of Solomon, yet these people would not listen to the promised Messiah. Jesus also showed them that they were not willing to believe in their hearts that which they were seeing with their eyes. This resulted in darkness and judgment.

We are like these people when we read His Word and reject that which we read and that which the Spirit reveals for our lives. If we don't like what we read or the direction of the Holy Spirit, we just ask for a sign so that we can do what we wanted to do all the time. Jesus doesn't seem to give much latitude concerning our response to truth. He says the eye is either single or it's evil. Paul said, "This one thing I do;" the Scriptures admonish us to seek first the Kingdom of God. We are also told to love the Lord with all our heart. Beware of signs; they are not always reliable. Check out the motive for asking for a sign from God.

INSIDE OUT

LUKE 11:37–54

How would you feel if someone served you a glass full of your favorite beverage in a lovely crystal glass with pure gold trim? Your pleasure in such a gesture would probably be turned to repulsion if a bug were floating on top and mold had grown on the inside edges of the glass. You would probably lose interest in the outside beauty of the glass and long for a plain, ordinary glass that had been washed to a sparkling, sanitary clean. In this case you would be more interested in cleanliness from the inside out. Jesus used this type of illustration to show that God is also more interested in our cleanliness from the inside out.

We can look just right on Sunday morning, saying the right things, singing the right songs, and praying prayers that sound just right. At the same time we can be dirty on the inside, and nobody will know— except God and maybe a close friend or member of our family. We can go a step further, perfecting the ritual of worship and the actions of our everyday lives to the point that we become like the scribes and Pharisees to whom Jesus spoke, seemingly perfect on the outside but dead and rotting on the inside. Like the Pharisees and lawyers on this account, we can, and do, lead others down this deceptive path as we strive to make them conform to "our doctrine" of do's and don'ts. Jesus rebuked these people harshly, but His motive, as always, was to reveal sin in their lives and show them the truth, giving them an opportunity for repentance and cleansing.

We need the same treatment when we harbor lust, bitterness, resentment, rebellion, jealousy, envy, etc., yet go our way with a form of worship. We become preoccupied with perfecting how we appear to people while we pass over the more important discipline of obedience to His Word and response to His love. What we need is cleansing from the inside out.

THERE ARE NO SECRETS

LUKE 12:1–12

How many times have we confided in someone by sharing a special secret? How many times have we been shocked to find that our secret had leaked out and was now known by many people? We all recall times as a child when we did something wrong, and yet we were confident that no one would find out. It seemed almost spooky when our parents somehow found out and confronted us with the details of the situation. How could they have known? We knew that a little bird didn't really tell them.

Jesus told the multitude that there were no secrets as far as God was concerned. He taught that not only does God know our dark, best-kept secrets now but that these secrets will be made known to all. This is a frightening thing to someone who is running from God, to someone who has rejected His son, Jesus, to someone who is rebelling against His will for his life. Jesus said that we should be afraid because God has the power, not only to make these secrets known, but also to punish us for our rebellion.

The good news is that this same, all-knowing God is interested in becoming our Heavenly Father so that He can forgive all our sins and do a positive, open work in our lives. If we confess to Jesus, receive Him as personal Savior, and let Him be Lord of our lives, He will put all these secret sins behind and remember them no more. Furthermore, He promises to live in us in the person of the Holy Spirit. He promises to so empower us that we can boldly represent Him before the powers of this earth.

Either our secrets will be made known as we stand before God, or He will put them under the blood of Jesus. In either case, there are no secrets, and the choice is ours.

Just A Few Dollars More

Luke 12:13–21

It is so easy to become preoccupied with the material things of this life. The drive to have more and more seems alive and well in all of humanity. The rich, the poor, and all those in between push and shove to get a few dollars more, so that they can buy more things or enlarge the base of operation so that more money can be accumulated. This drive can and will become a trap. When we have enough to meet our needs, and yet we become preoccupied with making more, having more, and spending more, we are trapped. If we find ourselves plotting and scheming to get more when we should be enjoying our family, friends, work, or a time alone with God, we are in danger.

In this passage the first man asked Jesus to help him get something that belonged to his brother. To want that which belongs to another is covetousness and against God's plan for our life. This is a rejection of God's promise to supply all our needs in accordance with His wealth. Beware of wanting a few dollars more that belong to someone else.

The second man was already rich and had plenty. Then he became preoccupied with having more. He seemed to want more just to store it up and have it on hand. Beware of wanting a few dollars more just to store up and have for the sake of having.

This second man also seemed to have reached the point in life where his trust was in his possessions. He had to have a few dollars more before he could put his soul at rest and "enjoy life." This is like the man who set his goal on riches and devoted all his time and energy toward this goal at the expense of time with family, friends, and God. At the end of life it is said that he had successfully climbed the ladder to reach his goal only to find that the ladder was leaning on the wrong building. As he climbed, he lost his family, his health and his soul—and all for a few dollars more.

MIND SET AND TREASURE HUNT

LUKE 12:22–40

Life is much more than what you eat and what you wear. We must not get caught up and become preoccupied with what we are accumulating (storing up) and how we look. Rather, we are to set a top priority on seeking the kingdom of heaven. These other things will fall in place, and they will not control us, but we will control them in the light of God's kingdom. God wants this for us. Jesus said that He came so that we "might have life and have it more abundantly."

The key is in where our heart is, for our heart will always be preoccupied with our true treasure. If you want to know where your treasure is, record the preoccupation of your heart each day. What do you plot, plan, scheme, and dream about during the day? If Jesus returned and played back an audio/video tape of our thoughts and meditations during the day before He arrived, what would it reveal as our treasure? "For where a man's treasure is, there is his heart also."

Jesus said that we were to store up treasures in heaven where they would last forever. He also warned that the treasures we store up here on earth will surely rust, decay and fail. This is totally opposite to what the world says. The world says that we should eat, drink, and be merry because it's all over when we die. The world says that we are to get all we can, can all we get, and sit on the can.

It is amazing that we are allowed to store up treasures in heaven. It is even more amazing that God has promised to provide all our needs here on earth when we set our mind, heart, and energy on the things of His kingdom. It is even more amazing that we can share with others from the abundance of His provision and get credit on our account in heaven. On what is our mind set in our treasure hunt?

QUESTIONS AND ANSWERS ABOUT TREASURES

LUKE 12:41–48

Peter's question was, "Are you addressing this parable about the treasures and stewardship and accountability to us or everyone?" Jesus' answer was: To both the "servant" who knows much and the one who knows little. The "faithful and wise" steward will be put in responsible charge of the Master's business which will be a test of the servant's evaluation of "true treasures." This test is measured by the "servant's" attention and prioritizing these responsibilities. The lord of the steward will surely return, evaluate accurately and reward or judge according to the job that is done.

In response to the servant's stewardship over "His household," the Master will either give him the "rule" over "all that He has" or beat him with many stripes. The key here is that the servant knew "His will" and yet did nothing about it (went after other treasures, v.47). The servant who did not know better shall be beaten with "few stripes" for not doing the Master's will. This is just, for surely a servant in the midst of the Master's business and everyday affairs should make it his priority (treasure) to study, learn and respond to the Master's will for his life. Jesus said, "And to whom much is given, much is required."

Where does that put us? Very simply, we must be obedient to that which we know. We are to diligently seek God's will for our life through the study of the Scriptures, prayer and regular attendance of worship services where truth is presented. We are to act on the truth we know and seek to know more truth, so we can respond in obedience. The trouble with most of us is that we already know more truth than we are acting upon. Why should God show us more truth when we do not apply the truth we know? Adrian Rogers brought this out in one of his sermons when he pointed out that light rejected brings more darkness, while light acted upon brings more light.

CHOOSE UP SIDES OVER JESUS

LUKE 12:49–59

For Jesus to say He came to send fire on earth indicates that it was not then accomplished. This could mean that He came to accomplish those things which would later release the fire (Holy Spirit) on earth. Jesus said in John 16:7, "It is expedient for you that I go...so that the Holy Spirit can come." In John 14:18 Jesus says, "I will not leave you comfortless." Again, in John 16:7, He continues, "I will send the Comforter." To receive Jesus as Savior and Lord and to live with the influence of the Holy Spirit will produce conflict of interest and conflict of treasures and in the process produce conflicts between people.

In Jesus' day the conflict was between the self-righteous law keepers and those who received, by faith, the Messiah. So it is today—can I be saved by grace, or do I have to practice good deeds to balance out the evil in my life?

Another conflict comes when, as a Christian, the "fire" within directs me to do or not do something that is in conflict with the way of the world. This brings disagreement and many times a parting of the ways for families, business partners, and friends. Usually these conflicts involve those closest to us. It may be over a television program, a movie rating, social drinking, business practices, church involvement, friendship, etc. We tend to choose up sides over Jesus as these issues arrive.

Our most important responsibility is to respond to the direction of the Holy Spirit within, recognize His direction, and respond to His will while He is leading or else He will eventually deliver us to the magistrate for disciplinary action (vv.58-59). The Lord spoke to Paul on the road to Damascus asking him why he kicked against the goads. Jesus said that He did nothing on His own initiative, but only that which the Father told Him.

When we ignore the flash flood warning, the tornado warnings, and the freeze warnings we are asking for trouble. When we fail to respond to the direction of the Holy Spirit, no matter the cost, we are in trouble.

DISASTER OR NEGLECT

LUKE 13:1–5

When we see or hear of a death, a tragedy or a disaster we may wonder about the relationship of these people with God and His role in the disaster. So it has always been. Jesus appealed to this spiritual mentality as some people pondered the plight of some Galileans and Jerusalemites who had been brutally slain and painfully destroyed in an accident. This tragedy was heavy on their minds, and Jesus used it to teach a lesson.

Jesus taught that we should be concerned about this most important matter—have we repented of our sins? If not, a greater disaster awaits us. Jesus warned that we do not need to be afraid of those who kill the body and then can do no more, but rather we should fear Him who has power, after he has killed, to cast into hell. (Matthew 10:28, Luke 12:5)

Jesus also offered encouragement when He said, "Whosoever shall confess me before men, him will I confess also before the angels of God." The turning point is the recognition of sin in our life and the confession of that sin with accompanying repentance.

It is heartwarming to see or be a part of an effort to relieve the suffering which results from a great disaster. The tornado victims, the earthquake victims, the victims of a plane crash or a hurricane cause us to come forward with our greatest effort. There is no way that we will neglect to respond to these desperate needs. These disasters take first place in the news because people are interested.

There is a greater disaster going on every day, and very few seem to care. The world around us is dying without Jesus, yet we neglect to respond to this desperate need. We can all pray for those we know without the Savior. A good way to pray is to ask God to show them their sin and convince them of their need for repentance.

DO IT OR BE REPLACED

LUKE 13:6–9

Could it be that the fig tree (many times symbolic of Israel) is a Christian, the vineyard is where we live and operate on earth, the dresser is Jesus, and the owner of the vineyard is God the Father? This same analogy could be made with the church here on earth. What could Jesus be teaching in this example of the fig tree?

A pen is made to write with, a car is made to transport, and a fig tree is made to bear figs. A Christian is "made" to worship God, fellowship with Him, and conform to His image. We are predestined to "conform to the image of Christ." We were created in His image. Paul said, "Now I see through a glass darkly but then we will be like Him." In becoming like Him we will do certain things as a result of this after transformation: "By their fruits ye shall know them." "Beware of the leaven of the Pharisees which is hypocrisy" (pretending to be something you are not—a fig tree with leaves but no figs).

Basic, yet most violated of the Christ-indwelled life is humility. We are caught up in "our rights," "our wants," "our way," yet the Scriptures tell us, "Let this mind be in you which was also in Christ Jesus." Jesus, being God in the flesh, chose to humble himself and die on the cross. Beware, fig tree with leaves and no figs, Christian with no love, no humility, no burden for lost, no hunger for fellowship with Jesus, no desire for fellowship with other Christians. You may be replaced—dug up, destroyed, killed, made ineffective, and stripped of gifts.

Respond to the tender, loving care of the dresser as He carefully digs around the hard soil of your heart and fertilizes your spirit with His words in the hope that you will be fruitful in all good works. Everything was provided to make the fig tree productive. Everything is also provided for us to be fruitful for Him—do it or be replaced.

People Or Piety, That Is The Question

Luke 13:10–17

Nothing is mentioned about anybody's faith in this passage. It doesn't even say whether or not the woman was looking for Jesus. He saw her, and He called to her. She could not even straighten up to look at Him.

He healed her for two reasons: first, to show the compassion of a loving, observant, caring Lord; second, to expose the cold hypocrisy of the pious law keeper who put the watering of animals above the healing of a poor wretch who had been in pain and despair for eighteen years.

The Pharisees modified the Sabbath law to say that any healing could be done in six days and not on the Sabbath. Consider this version of law: the donkey could be watered if he was thirsty, but people could suffer through the Sabbath. When Jesus exposed the heartless interpretation of this law, "All His adversaries were shamed."

We have stretched our "law" to do most anything we want on Sunday (the Lord's Day), but do we visit, witness, pray, share, worship, meditate, lead our families in a calm, relaxed spiritual experience? Is it piety or people that we are concerned about? It is easy to become so bound up in meetings and church work on Sunday that we have no time for rest, relaxation, and time with our family. This should be "prime time" when we can carry on a conversation or discuss our differences and difficulties without the pressures of business as usual.

I remember the Sundays of long ago when grandparents, uncles and aunts, cousins, or neighbors would come by our house. We would eat and play or visit and talk. What happened to the day of rest set aside by the Lord? We tend to wear ourselves out on weekends to the point that we have to go back to work to recover. What better time is there to think about the problems of others and lift them up in prayer? What better time to call, visit, or write a note, to encourage and edify those God places on our hearts? Piety or people, that is the question.

GOD'S KINGDOM, CONTAMINATED

LUKE 13:18–19

The mustard seed is so small! But within it, dormant and waiting, is a large tree. A tree that grows big casts a shadow over the garden, restricting sunlight necessary for the growth of vegetation below. It catches the rain from heaven before it can reach the flowers below, spreads its root system to extend as far out as its "drip line," thereby taking the nourishment from the plants of the garden. It spreads its branches high and wide to provide protection and permanent residence for the fowls of the air who destroy the plants of the garden and eat up the seeds dropped from the plants, thereby disrupting the cycle of reproduction within the garden.

Our back yard has many oak trees, and I have seen this process occur. The carpet grass is starved out and literally dies from lack of sunlight, rain and nourishment. It all started from a few small acorns. The grackles gather in the trees, dig in the grass, scratch in the garden area, and continue the cycle of destruction and distraction in the midst of the yard and garden.

So it is with a "little sin" in the midst of God's kingdom. A little giving of ground as a nation in the areas of drugs, pornography, homosexuality, divorce, living together outside marriage, immorality, etc. and a beautiful nation becomes contaminated, dying, decaying and departing from that for which it was established under God.

So it is with a church, a denomination, or an individual's life. A little sin planted in the midst of a perfect garden will grow and grow until the effects are felt throughout. The garden, the nation, the life of the individual all belong to God; therefore, He should be consulted for instruction about planting, cultivating and the growth of each. "Whatsoever a man soweth, that shall he also reap." Consult with the Master Gardener of life before you do much planting in your life. The harvest may come late, but it will come, and it will always be more than was planted.

A Little Sin Goes A Long Way

Luke 13:20–22

The parable of the leaven is similar to the parable of the mustard seed. It is interesting to notice that the "measures of meal" got there first, before the leaven. The other ingredients were put in, mixed and kneaded to form an uncontaminated lump. At this point the leaven was "hid" in the mix and the process started. Contamination took place, beginning with that which was in contact with the leaven and then spreading until the entire lump or mix was contaminated.

The unusual thing about yeast is that once it has worked, no process of separation is available. The mix is forever. It can be allowed to spend itself and the effect is reduced, but the consequences are there. The bread may not rise as much, but there is a taste. This phenomenon can be applied to the church or to the Christian life. A little sin goes a long way.

It could start with an individual in the church and spread to those closest to him and continue on until the entire church is contaminated. The best remedy is to remove the leaven immediately when it is recognized. The same is true with sin in our lives—confess quickly, repent and modify (remove) any lifestyle that supports this sin tendency.

Interestingly enough, this process is also depictive of the influence of the indwelling Spirit as a result of salvation. The Holy Spirit "contaminates" us within and spreads throughout our lives. The Spirit never gives up. He is always working, probing, and quietly pleading, and He cannot be removed once we are saved. The Holy Spirit can be "spent" or quenched by rejection and by the willful lack of response on our part.

"One bad apple will contaminate the whole barrel," as the saying goes. The Bible says, "I will send the Spirit of Truth...He will be in you and teach you all things...quench not the Spirit...My Spirit will not always strive with man." Do not sin against God by rejecting the Holy Spirit. Let Him have His way in your life so that every area of your life is influenced by Him.

PASSWORD TO HEAVEN

LUKE 13:23–30

There are few that can be saved! The Bible teaches that the way is straight and there are few that enter. Jesus said to "strive" to enter at the "straight gate." There will come a time when no one may enter and not another one will be saved. God warned, "I will not always strive with man."

It is unforgivable to "blaspheme the Holy Spirit," that is to usurp the power and authority of the Holy Spirit. One should never say, "Spirit, leave me alone. I do not accept this Jesus, and I do not accept your authority to reveal Him to me." The story is told of a man who once experienced the powerful influence of the Holy Spirit, urging him to repent of his sins and trust Jesus as Savior and Lord. He rejected this influence, and over the years it never came again. He shared this story as he lay dying and told the one witnessing to him. "I cannot trust Jesus now. I've never had the desire since that time He urged me many years ago."

When the door is closed, either by the withdrawal of the Holy Spirit in this age or by the end design of God at the end of this age, no one else shall get in. Many will try, offering up all sorts of pleadings relative to their "association with" the Lord. But the key is do you know Him, and more importantly does He know you? It will not matter how much you know about Him or how well you know others who belong to Him.

There is only one way into the gate. That is with the password - Jesus! What will you say when the Lord asks, "Why should I let you into My heaven?" Jesus said, "I am the Way, the Truth and the Life; no man cometh to the Father but by Me." Anyone may come - from north, south, east or west. The Bible says, "Whosoever will may come." But it also says that a personal relationship with Jesus is the key that unlocks the door. Receive Him as your personal Savior and invite Him in to be Lord of your life. Tomorrow may be too late.

PERSPECTIVES AND PRIORITIES

LUKE 13:31–35

Jesus, being warned that Herod would kill Him, began to review the chain of events that were soon to take place in His life at Jerusalem. As He remembered the prophets killed in Jerusalem and contemplated His own fate, He became burdened over the great city. He wept and longed to see the city come to Him and receive Him as Messiah and Savior. Rejection by His own special people, the Jews, seemed to hurt Him more than the cross.

He likened Himself to a mother hen and Jerusalem to the baby chicks. When it rains, the mother hen clucks, squats, and lifts her wings slightly so that the chicks can gather under her warm body and be protected from the rain by her wings. The little chickens will literally drown standing in the rain if they don't take to the shelter offered. Some of the chicks don't come to the mother hen even though they are very near to her. They hear the beckoning of their loving mother but somehow reject this lifesaving call.

Jesus' perspective was on the agony He would suffer, but His priority was fixed on the needy "chicks" of Jerusalem and the fate of that great city. Sometimes the best cure for our own hurts is to focus on the needs of others. We must see and feel the lostness of those about us who are dying spiritually even though they live physically. We must remember that the Savior is always near, gently calling and pleading.

When our perspectives and priorities are aligned with His, we will become active in His cause. We will recognize the inner calling and respond to the insistent directing of the Christ who lives within.

LEGALLY RIGHT BUT TOTALLY WRONG

LUKE 14:1–6

The Pharisees invited Jesus so they could watch Him. I wonder if they invited the man with dropsy also? It appears to be a planned situation to test Jesus. No one spoke, so He read their thoughts and intentions. Jesus went straight to the point. The Pharisees thought they planned it, but Jesus took command of the occasion and the situation to once again show them that legally right from man's perspective can be totally wrong from God's perspective.

The question? Was healing on the Sabbath legal? Jesus changed the question to deal with a more important matter. Is man's relation to man and God more important than the strict keeping of the Law (established by man)? What is more important, man or beast? Jesus showed that they had become so legal that they missed the Messiah and made laws that missed the heart of God.

We should always be aware that wherever we are, as Christians, we are being watched. Many situations present opportunities for a course of action that demonstrates our faith and commitment to Jesus. We must go a step further and take command of the situation at all times. By the power of the Word and the Holy Spirit, we will recognize opportunities to demonstrate His sufficiency, His power, His joy, and His reality in our lives.

A little boy decided he could fool the wise old man who had the reputation of knowing all things and being all wise. The boy devised a plan and caught a bird which he held in his hands before the old man. He asked the old man, "Is the bird dead or alive?" intending to crush the bird if the answer were "alive" and release him if the answer were "dead." The wise old man looked into the boy's heart and answered, "My son, the bird is alive or dead, whichever you want him to be."

We are "alive" or "dead" to the circumstances around us whichever we choose. Jesus encouraged us not to worry about what we will say in time of testing, promising that the Spirit will give us utterance from the Word.

LIFT YOURSELF UP AND ANOTHER WILL PUT YOU DOWN

LUKE 14:7–11

Apparently the building used for weddings had rooms located at different levels. The host would place the invited guests at different levels, depending on the degree of honor due each, with the highest honored guest at the top level. Visualize an open patio area with rooms on several levels around it.

The picture in this scripture is of one who has elevated himself in his own eyes such that, as an invited guest, he assumes that surely no other will be of higher honor than himself, and so he seats himself in the highest room. Later, the host escorts one of higher honor to that room and, to the humiliation of the first man, he must give up his seat and move to the lowest level.

This is pictured in the television commercial when the former baseball player seats himself in the coveted box seats down front near the batters' box only to be removed by an usher who escorts the people down who have the tickets for that box of seats. The former player ends up in the "crow's roost" at the top of the stadium.

Jesus teaches that we should humble ourselves and take the lowest seat. If we are to be honored, let the host decide where we should sit. The Bible is very clear on this matter. "Humble yourselves therefore, under the mighty hand of God, that you may be exalted in due time." "The last shall be first and the first shall be last." "Let this mind be in you which was also in Christ Jesus." Jesus, who humbled himself to death on the cross, said, "I am not to be served but to serve."

There are two basic principles here. First, we are to humble ourselves. God will provide plenty of opportunities and situations for us to humble ourselves, but it is up to us to humble ourselves from within. Secondly, if we are due honor, it will come from another through God. He will exalt us in due time, and it will usually bring more honor to Him than to ourselves.

GUEST LIST FROM GOD

LUKE 14:12–14

Jesus encouraged His host to avoid inviting people that would be considered relatives, rich friends or "brothers" (same race or belief). These would be able to pay him back by inviting him to dinner. The advice here is to invite the undesirable, the unwanted, the sick, the poor, and the crippled. There is no way this group could pay you back. But God will pay you back at the resurrection of the just. In one case, treasures are stored up in earth, and in the other, treasures are stored in heaven.

Whom do we invite to our home or out to dinner? Isn't it mostly those who invite us to their home, or those who can help further a business deal or give us advice or counsel about a certain matter? Our homes should be open to our friends and relatives, but we should also welcome the lost, the down and out, those who are struggling.

We like to say that God "gave us" our home, but do we use it to His honor and glory? Our home should be used as a place to share our faith in Jesus Christ. It should be a place of refuge and encouragement to all who come. Who were your last house guests? When is the last time you shared your faith with another at your home? Do people come by expecting the presence of God to be evident?

"Store not up for yourselves treasures on earth...but store up treasures in heaven." If our actions are motivated to please or influence man, we receive our reward from man. But if we are motivated to please God, our reward is in heaven, and we have peace that passes understanding here and now! We can store up riches in heaven by the way we share our home here on earth.

RSVP: Invitation Declined

Luke 14:15–24

It appears that the one who spoke presupposed that because he was a Jew, of the seed of Abraham, he had a reservation to eat bread at the table in God's kingdom. As he pondered how great it was going to be as an honored part of God's kingdom, Jesus posed a parable. In the parable, not only were the guests invited, but they were also personally reminded of the event by the host's servant.

However, they gave many excuses, most of which were related to the press of daily business (new land purchase, purchasing oxen). When the host heard these excuses, he opened the banquet to everyone. The servant was sent to compel them to come, but only until the house was full.

This could be a picture of the Pharisees, scribes, priests, and devout Jews who felt that, because they were descendants of Abraham, they had a guaranteed place in God's kingdom. Jesus pointed out in the parable that you can only be a part of God's kingdom by invitation, and the Jews had the first invitation personally extended to them by the Passover Lamb of God, even Jesus.

They refused, for the most part, and God extended the invitation to all people, no matter what their position in life. Note that after some of them refused, the servant compelled, pleaded, and urged others until the house was full. Then, none of those invited earlier could come.

This shows that "now is the day of salvation." "Now is the accepted time." "My Spirit will not always strive with man." When Jesus calls, we had better come! The house may become full today and after that the invitation is no more. Respond to the Savior's invitation now. Is it accepted or declined?

ALL OR NOTHING AT ALL

LUKE 14:25–35

Great numbers of people followed after Jesus as His fame spread across the land. Knowing the shallowness of most hearts and understanding the selfish motives that brought many to Him, He emphasized the cost of following close to Him as a disciple.

Taking up your cross is to deny anything that is not His will for your life. It is living the Spirit-filled life. Jesus said that He did nothing except that which the Father told Him to do. So it must be with us. We must know His will for our lives and do it!

Knowing His will is difficult for most of us. However, we can know His will by considering three things: (I) circumstances, such as a chain of events, open doors, closed doors; (2) a word from God, coming from His Word; (3) our agreeing spirit. For these things to be effective in our lives, we must be consistently in His Word and continually in prayer and meditation. Without regular attendance in a Bible-teaching, preaching, worshipping Church; without a private, personal, intimate time everyday in God's Word; and without a regular time set aside in serious prayer, we cannot know for sure what God's will is for our lives.

Beware if God seems to tell you things that conflict with each other over a short period of time. I have heard people say, "God told me to do this or that," only to find that a few months later God had told them something else. God is not confused. He is orderly—the same yesterday, today, and tomorrow.

When I was a boy, I would go swimming in the Big Elkhart Creek with the plow hands. After work, we ran to the water, still cold from the spring time. Some would plunge in, while others would test the water with a foot and stand, shivering on the bank. Those who stayed on the bank were cold and uncomfortable, while those in the creek became climatized to the water.

So it is with our commitment to the will of God. Once we get a word from Him, the circumstances line up, and our inner spirit agrees with His Spirit. We must plunge in and let Him climatize us to walking in His way.

GOOD SHEPHERDING

LUKE 15:1–7

Jesus' messages and His willingness to minister to all without preference to social or religious status drew "publicans and sinners" to Him. They came because they knew they were welcome, and they knew they had a need. They came because He went out first to them.

Note the first word of vs. 1. "Then." After Jesus showed His heart toward them they came to Him. He received them, and this caused murmuring among the religious bunch.

The parable of the lost sheep shows the heart of God toward every single person. He left the ninety and nine to go look for the one lost sheep. The ninety and nine could stick together, support each other and provide help for each other until the shepherd returned. The one had lost his sense of direction and had become unaware of the danger about him.

The shepherd's friends rejoiced over the return of the lost sheep. Maybe Jesus was saying to the Pharisees, "You are not my friends because you have not a heart for the lost." They had lost their compassion for the outsider. They had become so caught up in the letter of the law that they had missed the love of God expressed in the person of Jesus Christ.

This parable would also place them in the category of the lost sheep. Jesus had spent much time in the presence of the scribes and Pharisees sharing the Word, teaching parables, pleading with them, rebuking them and showing them that He was the promised Messiah. They had lost their sense of direction. Thinking they were right left them in a dangerous position.

Jesus never gave up on anyone. He was always willing to go and minister to needs around Him. We must follow the example of the Good Shepherd and minister to those around us, regardless of their position in life. We should have an inner compelling to rejoice over the salvation of one. We should have an inner drive to always be looking for the one that is lost.

FIRST THINGS FIRST

LUKE 15:8–10

This parable shows the effort to recover or retain material possessions. It also shows the relief, excitement and joy of finding or recovering the threatened material possession. Our possessions represent hard labor and concerted effort.

The following questions are crucial. How much effort do we make toward "finding" a lost person and showing him Christ and His salvation? How much effort do we make to help restore a brother or sister who is out of fellowship? How much joy is stirred up inside us when we see the "lost" get saved, the "backslidden" restored? How much excitement is generated when someone shares how his friend or relative has been saved?

Jesus gave a stern rebuke as He spoke to the religious crowd, "But woe unto you, Pharisees! You tithe mint and rue and all manner of herbs and pass over the love of God. These things ought you to have done, and not to leave the other undone." The Bible speaks of a bad heart condition, "You have a form of worship, but your hearts are far from Me." First things first: "Seek ye first the kingdom of God and all these things shall be added unto you."

Someone has said that we can tell where our heart is by identifying the things with which we are preoccupied. We can also evaluate our priorities by honestly listing those things that excite our heart the most. A measure of what is most important in our lives can be determined by the amount of self-discipline we apply in certain areas of our life.

Would we rather be watching television than spending time with our family? Would we rather be fishing or playing golf than going to church? Who are our prayers focused on—ourselves or others? First things first.

THE LIFE OF ANOTHER CHANCE

LUKE 15:11–19

This parable shows the foolishness of the youthful mind. That is why God expects children to be under their parents' authority until they are able to go out on their own. At one stage in life a young person thinks Mom and Dad are stupid, or at best, old-fashioned and do not understand them.

Off on his own to enjoy life, the boy in the parable soon learned that all is not as it appears to be. He did not have the maturity of discernment to see through "would-be friends" who were only with him until the money ran out.

When this Jewish boy hit bottom and had to work with pigs in order to survive, he reflected on the way it was back home. Suddenly he realized that his dad was not as old-fashioned as he once thought. He began to see how his father cared for those under his authority. The young man also recognized that his father treated the hired hands better than he was being treated.

This shows a beautiful relationship between the boy and his dad in that he felt free to go back home to apologize and confess his actions as sin, expecting to be forgiven. Note the humble spirit when the boy said, "Make me as one of your servants." The relationship built over the years between father and son brought about this satisfying conclusion.

How about it? Will you be the first one your children think of after they have left the nest and hit a difficult situation in life? Will you be the first to know? Do they feel comfortable in apologizing, confessing, and expecting your help and understanding? Have they grown to respect your leadership and wisdom enough to ask your help and counsel in a difficult situation?

This is how parents should be toward their children because it is a picture of how our Heavenly Father is towards us. He guarantees us another chance when we place our trust in His Son Jesus Christ. When we fail as Christians, He offers us another chance because the Bible says that if we confess our sins, He is faithful and just to forgive us.

CONFESSIONS AND REPENTANCE

LUKE 15:20–21

So many times we confess to God or to one another and say, "I'm sorry." But how often is our conscience cleared without a real commitment to turn away from repeating the same offense?

Here is the story of a young man who "came to himself," realized the error of his ways and then "he arose and came to his father." I remember counseling with a couple about to get a divorce, and at one point in our discussion about God's plan for a marriage to be until death, one party said, "I've already confessed this as sin and God has forgiven me."

The Scriptures do say, "If we confess our sin, He is faithful and just to forgive us our sin," but the Scriptures also say, "Except you repent, you shall all likewise perish and bring forth fruit worthy of your repentance." Does not the admonition of our Lord to take up your cross imply the yielding of our will and personal desire to that of the indwelling Lord? When we confess our sins, He is not only "faithful" but also "just" in His forgiveness. Justice demands that we also repent and turn from this sin.

In another similar counseling situation, one party said, "I know it's wrong, but I'm tired of talking." Notes were written to some of the family members apologizing for the hurt after the divorce. But where is the repentance? Where is the effort to work it out through counseling? James wrote, questioning the good of faith that did not produce works, and other scriptures teach that confession without repentance is also dead.

This story speaks of a young man whose repentance matched his confession. He confessed his sin against God and his father and then began to do something about it. Confession and repentance cannot be separated, according to the Scriptures. Confession is an act of humility and repentance is a commitment of faith to change our way in His strength. Both build Christian character.

Forgiving, Forgetting And Rejoicing

Luke 15:22–24

Someone has said, "You can forgive but you can't forget." This is true to a point. Only God can forget. "I will remove your sins as far as the east is from the west, and remember them no more." We cannot completely forget , but when the person, situation, or circumstance wounds us, we have two choices. One choice is to let it control our thought and relive it with all the associated hurting actions and reactions. The alternative is to reject the thoughts from our mind as soon as they come. We can remember God and what He has done for us. We can recall what satan wants to do to us. We have the power to refuse to dwell on the bitterness. Soon the details will fade, and the power it holds on our life will be gone.

The father made up his mind to forgive the young son even before he returned. He was watching, hoping, praying, believing that the son would return. He saw the son while "he was yet a great way off." This speaks to the faith of the father in God's promise, "Bring up a child in the way he should go and when he is old he will not depart...." I can hear the father praying after his son had left his influence and protection, "Dear God, bless the boy for I have raised him as best I could under Your Word. I have made many mistakes and errors, but one thing I did right, I committed him to You before he was born and have recommitted him to You many times since. He is Yours. Do with him as You please, but I beseech Thee, oh Father, protect him against harm, from the evil one, turn his heart to Yourself, and bring him home."

The father looked down the road every day, believing that God was faithful. One day he saw the boy coming home after God had done His work in the boy's life. Note that the father did not scold the boy. He had a deep, personal relationship with God and knew that the boy had been disciplined with perfection. He probably recalled a similar incident in his own life when God had chastened him. He simply forgave, forgot, and rejoiced in the return of the boy and in the assurance of what God had done in the boy's life.

TESTING THE HEART

LUKE 15:25–32

What about the son that stayed at home, obeyed his father, worked hard and conformed to the family mold? Any father would be proud to have a son like this, never transgressing and always serving in the family tradition. But there was a heart problem.

Outwardly, the older son appeared to be almost perfect, but this was only skin deep. Down inside, he hated his younger brother. Note verse 29 regarding the "I's" and then verse 30 regarding "thy son," not my brother. It seemed almost like the older son was obedient to his father and worked hard for selfish reasons. He expected special attention for his work even though he would inherit most of the family wealth under Jewish law.

God points out in His Word that the heart is "desperately wicked" and "who can know it." Again He said that some worship Him with their actions, but their hearts are far from Him. "Man looketh on the outward appearance but God looketh upon the heart."God is concerned about our heart because He knows that "as a man thinketh in his heart, so is he." Paul wrote, "without love, I am nothing." He must have known that love is the true test of what a man really is.

Note the father's patience and perspective. Remember, he said, you are here with me, and we enjoy each other's fellowship. All that I have is yours. But more important than all this, be happy and rejoice, for "this thy brother was dead and is alive again, was lost but now is found." It was important for the older son to see the younger boy as his brother, not as his father's other son.

We can easily take the heart test. Simply check our heart's reaction to the success of others, to the favor received by another from one we love, to the salvation and restoration of a brother and sister, to the victory of our friends and associates. Beware of coverings that hide the true feelings of our heart.

WORD WISE, HEAVEN DUMB

LUKE 16:1-18

This is a strange parable, but the message it conveys is very profound. A man was caught wasting his boss's goods. To protect himself, he changed the balance due on the debt of those who owed the boss. In so doing, they would become obligated to him and take him in once he was fired. Even his boss commended him on this sly but wise action.

Jesus pointed out that "the children of the world," such as these two characters, were wiser than the "children of light." This is probably directed toward the Pharisees, since they were in charge of the things of God (Boss) and were "wasting" it. They rejected Christ, changed the laws to suit their needs, and had no love or compassion for the people. Jesus warned them that they had better make friends with the world, for the Boss was going to fire them, and they would have no place with Him. Therefore, they should make their eternity with the children of the world.

The Pharisees had not been faithful with what they had—the law of Moses and the promise of the Messiah, handed down by the prophets. Because of this, God could not trust them with the New Testament— the age of grace through the Messiah, Jesus Christ. They knew the scriptures as scholars, but missed the Christ of the very Scriptures they mastered.

This is also a warning to us: Do not get carried away with the things of the world and neglect the great salvation story. God has committed to us the good news of the New Testament, which is salvation by grace through Christ. Let us go about being good stewards of it. It is impossible to go both ways at the same time; we cannot serve two masters. We must plunge in like children at a swimming pool on a spring day when the water is still cold. Once climatized to the water, it becomes invigorating. So will it be for us as we share the good news of Christ in our daily walk and witness.

REAL LIFE IS AFTER DEATH

LUKE 16:19–31

The age-old question is: "If a man dies, will he live again?" Jesus spoke of this in this parable. He also alluded to the fact that we are all living our lives either God's way or man's way. The story emphasizes the validity and accuracy of the Word of God. Jesus also showed that we must make up our minds and hearts now, in this life, for it will be too late in the real life which is yet to come.

Jesus emphasized that from man's point of view, the rich man had it all and the beggar had nothing. Man looks at outward things, but God looks on the heart. Note that both men die, as we all must die (if Jesus does not come first), and our eternal destiny is carried out at that time.

There is no way to get from the place of the beggar's spirit to the place of the rich man's spirit. A "great gulf fixed" between them, and there can be no passage between the two. Neither can there be communication between the living and the dead. Beware of those who communicate with the dead!

Most importantly, notice that there is no way to change our eternal destiny after death. The rich man repented and had true compassion for the lost that were left behind, but he remained in hell. Those who remained behind had the same opportunity that the rich man had—the Word of God, the preachers, the teachers and the tugging of the Spirit of God on their hearts as they stepped over the beggars along life's way.

We also face beggars along our road of life, those who only want a crumb of truth or a bit of help from our table of plenty. Real life begins at death. This life is simply a time to prepare for the next life. All preparation must be made now; it cannot be made after this life is over. It all begins with what we do with Jesus, the One who came back from the dead to show us the way of eternal life.

FORGIVENESS IS GODLINESS

LUKE 17:1-6

Once, Peter asked Jesus how many times he should forgive his brother, seven times? Jesus replied that Peter should forgive him seventy times seven. Forgive without end, that is true forgiveness, and that is the way God forgives. Forgiveness is godliness.

There is one small prerequisite to forgiveness, however, and that is repentance. The Bible says that if we confess our sin, He is faithful and just to forgive our sins and cleanse us from all unrighteousness. In this story, Jesus said, "If he repents, forgive him." As many times as he repents, we are to forgive him.

Most Christians are willing to repent and to forgive, but few are willing to "rebuke thy brother" if he trespasses against them. We are somehow intimidated by having to face a brother with his sins. This action, however, is a wonderful opportunity to pray and discuss a wrong with a brother. The Bible says that if a brother is restored, a multitude of sins is covered. When we discuss sin with a brother, we gain insight into his life. We learn of his good and bad points, and, in short, we really get to know him. It may also reveal sin or weakness in our own lives. It will certainly make us more sensitive to those about us.

The practice of rebuking, repenting and forgiving takes faith that God will honor that which he told us to do. The main objective is forgiveness, which is godliness. We are not to be judgmental or condemning in our approach. We are to look for an opportunity to forgive and encourage, even as Christ forgives and encourages us.

Our response to repentance clearly must be forgiveness. We don't need to pray about when someone comes in repentance asking our forgiveness. We need to pray very much before we rebuke someone. Our motive and a confidence in God's directing must be sure.

MEDALS ARE FOR "ABOVE AND BEYOND"

LUKE 17:7–10

It is the duty of every soldier to defend his country and do whatever his commander says, even in the face of death. But occasionally a soldier will step out beyond the command of this authority and, at a greater risk of his life, do a brave deed. For this, he may get a medal inscribed, "For bravery above and beyond the call of duty."

Jesus likened his disciples to servants. In this example, the servant had plowed in the fields all day, which was also his duty. He had fed the livestock, which was his duty. When he came home, he had another duty: to prepare and feed his master before he could eat.

Jesus then said that when we keep all the definite, indisputable commandments, we have simply done our duty and could be called unprofitable. Sometimes we must go beyond our duty as illustrated by the words of Paul: "I will eat no meat or do anything that will cause my brother to stumble. I am all things to all men, that I might win some." An opportunity to influence someone to make a saving commitment for Christ should be acted upon, no matter the risk.

We must move into the arena that requires faith in our God to get the victory. "Don't worry," Jesus said, "of what you shall say when you stand before kings, for in that hour it will be given you." Worship, study and pray that we will be ready to move out, as the brave soldier, when the opportunity comes to go above and beyond the call of duty.

The soldier who wins the medal usually acts without study or thought of the consequences. The training along with the dedication and devotion to the cause spark the brave action. Our walk with God along with our dedication and devotion to His cause will spark our action for his cause.

WHOLE IS MORE THAN HEALED

LUKE 17:11–19

Jesus was not being bound by tradition or prejudice whenever he went through Samaria, which was avoided by most Jews. On one occasion He encountered the woman at the well, and on this occasion he meets the ten lepers. In both cases, He used the occasion to show truth mingled with love and compassion.

All ten of the lepers cried out to Jesus for mercy, and all followed his instructions. They were all healed as they went their way to the priest, but only one returned to glorify God and thank Jesus. He was a Samaritan, an outcast in the sight of the Jews. I wonder if this Samaritan was the one who suggested that the lepers go to Jesus in the first place? A word of praise and thanks is recognition that we did not do it alone.

A father delights in giving and doing for his children, but what a joy it is when they thank him. So it is with God our Father. "By him therefore let us offer the sacrifice of praise to God continually that is the fruit of our lips giving thanks to His name." (Heb. 13:15) The practice of giving thanks to God for all things is an expression of our faith in Him and our gratitude.

It is interesting to note that Jesus said, "Arise, go thy way: thy faith hath made thee whole." The man was already healed, as were the other nine. What did Jesus mean, "made whole?" I think it means he was saved by God's grace as he responded to the revelation of Jesus, the Messiah, the Son of God, even God himself, and acknowledged this with a loud voice. Only then was he made whole. Being whole is more than being healed.

We desperately plead with God for the physical healing of a friend or loved one, and we should do this. But how many lost friends and relations do we lift in prayer that they may be made whole by the Great Physician?

LOOKING FOR THAT WHICH IS ALL ABOUT

LUKE 17:20–21

Have you ever looked and looked for something that was lost, only to find that it was in your pocket or in your purse all the time? The Pharisees "demanded" that Jesus tell them when the kingdom of God would occur. Their concept of the coming of the kingdom of God was for the Messiah to come in great power and rule as King over Israel. They looked for things to be like they were during the rule of King David, only with a more powerful and blessed ruler, the Messiah.

Since Jesus claimed to be the Messiah, these skeptics demanded to know the time of the coming of the kingdom to discredit Him. They knew that Jesus could never occupy the throne of Israel and be the hard, fierce ruler they expected to liberate them from the Roman yoke. They didn't realize that they needed liberation from within.

Jesus answered by warning that they would not see the kingdom of God as a political party or as a revolutionary force led by the future king. He said, "the kingdom of God is within you." Within each of us is a void that only God can fill. There is a longing, a searching, a desperate desire to know what life is all about and who is in charge. There is also a desire to experience this great truth personally. There is a seeking to find that force or person that can provide the answers to this complex life.

A kingdom has a king and subjects. Jesus is the King, and we become His subjects when we respond to the revelation by the Holy Spirit that King Jesus is the Savior, our only hope. We respond by repenting of our sins, asking God's forgiveness, and receiving Jesus as our Savior. Then, as a guarantee of the Promise, the Holy Spirit lives in us, and the kingdom of God is within. We become His subjects with our lives controlled by the indwelling Christ, who sits on the throne of our life. The kingdom of God is within!

WHEN WILL HE COME BACK?

LUKE 17:22–37

This scripture deals with what is commonly referred to as, "the second coming of Christ." This is a worthy study that will take you beyond this devotional.

First, Jesus warns that we are not to be deceived by those who will say "go here" or "go there" to see the Lord's return. His return will be quick and dramatic, like the lightening that comes out of one part of the sky and lights up the whole heavens. The Bible teaches that no one knows the exact time of this event.

Jesus emphasized that before this can happen, He must be rejected and suffer. After all, without the suffering, death, and resurrection of Jesus, there would be no one to come back and no one to come back for. "I am the way, the truth, and the life; no man cometh unto the Father but by Me." He promised that He would come again and receive us so that we would be with Him.

Jesus indicated that the second coming will be like the times of Noah and Lot. Things will continue as usual: eating, drinking, marrying, selling, buying, building, and the normal hustle of life. Again, Jesus emphasized the suddenness of the event, "in the same day," with business as usual, it will happen. It will be similar to the moment of fire and brimstone on Sodom. There will be no time or desire to get our belongings. We go as we are, with no preparation, from work, from bed, from business as usual. We will not mind, and it will not matter unless, like Lot's wife, we are more concerned with remaining in the world than going. For those who know Him as Savior, rejoice, the day of our Lord is approaching with each tick of the clock.

PRAYER AND FAITH

LUKE 18:1–8

We have been bombarded with the power of positive determination. Corporations and organizations pay thousands of dollars to have a motivational speaker come and tell their people that they can accomplish anything with a set of priorities and an unfailing determination to do it. What they fail to tell them is that the cost of accomplishing this can be the loss of relationships with their family, friends and God. An attitude of winning at all costs will indeed cost you much.

The woman in this parable pursued her obsession for revenge with great determination. Many other things in her life must have suffered from neglect as she "troubled" the judge consistently. The Bible says, "He gave them the desire of their heart, but brought leanness to their soul."(Ps. 106:15) We must be sure that the desire of our heart is put there by God, and the priorities of our life are aligned with the Word and the direction of the Holy Spirit. "Delight thyself also in the Lord; and He shall give thee the desires of thine heart." (Ps. 37:4)

In effect, Jesus said that we need to be preoccupied with prayer, crying out to God day and night. This is an expression of faith, praying for God to provide us with that which He has already promised, although we have not yet seen it. Prayer is fellowship and friendship with God. It is the persistent expression of a needy heart to be in communion with Him. Even as we steadfastly strive in that which God desires us to accomplish, we must PRAY IN FAITH that it will be accomplished the way He wants it accomplished. We also must be willing to ask God to correct our course, if we have missed His will. This parable tells us that God will do it!

Our job is to find His will for our life by studying the Scripture and following the direction of the Holy Spirit. Then we are to continue in prayer and faith.

WHERE IS YOUR TRUST?

LUKE 18:9–14

One of the most thought-provoking questions I have ever heard is, "Suppose you were to die tonight and stand before God, and He were to ask you, 'Why should I let you into My heaven,' what would you say?" I have posed this question to many people and to my own heart. Much to my surprise, the answer is usually similar to the prayer of the Pharisee in this parable. The majority of people will say that they are not bad, that they are as good as the next person, that they have been baptized, that they are a good father or mother, or that they are a good provider. This is called self-righteousness, because their righteousness is related to their good deeds. Most people trust in the hope that God will weigh their good works against their bad deeds and the scales will tip in favor of their good deeds.

From the world's point of view, a Pharisee was righteous. They kept the law to the letter, but they had a "heart problem." They worshiped God with their actions, but their hearts were far from Him. They exalted themselves as if to say, "God, you have no choice but to save us; we are so good." However, Jesus told Nicodemus, the famous Pharisee, that he must be born again in order to see the kingdom of God. Jesus was teaching in this parable that there is only one way to come before God, with a bowed head and a humble heart, realizing that we are sinners at best, and that except for the mercy of God and the gift of salvation through Jesus Christ, we have no hope. We cannot compare ourselves to others as a measure of our goodness. The Bible says we are "all sinners." We must compare ourselves to Jesus. This will bring us to our knees, crying out for mercy, as did the publican.

When I get to heaven, if God asks me why He should let me in, I will have to answer, "All I have is Jesus. If what He did for me on the cross is not enough, I can't come in." My trust is in Jesus Christ alone. All my works and feeble efforts to be obedient to the tasks set out by my Lord are a simple "thank you" to Him who paid it all for me. Where is your trust?

CHILDREN KNOW THE WAY

LUKE 18:15–17

Children are so trusting and their faith is so complete. I remember one day, when my daughter was a little girl, the family was swimming at a public pool which had a high diving board. I dove off the high board, and she wanted to jump but was afraid. She climbed the ladder and walked out to the end of the board, and it was obvious that she was afraid. I swam to a point near where she would hit the water and said, "Go ahead and jump. I'll be right here." Without further hesitation, she jumped, not because her fear was gone, but because she had complete faith that her father would do what he promised.

In this account of Jesus with the children, two things stand out. First of all, He loves children and so should we. The Bible says, "Lo, children are a heritage of the Lord."(Ps 127:3) The Bible also says, that the man is blessed who has many children. Secondly, Jesus used the well-known trusting nature of a child to show how we all must come into the kingdom of God.

Grown-ups want to know all the answers before they trust, but this is not trust at all. Childlike trust comes by knowing enough about someone to believe in them for anything. This is not blind faith, but faith that is based on fact about a person, yet reaches beyond that which is fully known and understood.

Saving faith is trusting in Jesus Christ alone for our salvation. We don't know all the answers. If we did, we would not need faith. We do know that it is an historical fact that Jesus died on the cross for our sins, was buried and arose from the grave the third day. That is sufficient! All of the world's great heroes have died, and their graves are marked for us to see their accomplishments, but not so with Jesus. His tomb is empty. Even His critics are without explanation for this. Let us follow the children with complete faith in Jesus Christ alone. The children know the way.

WHY NOT TAKE ALL OF ME?

LUKE 18:18–30

There is an old love song that says, "Why not take all of me?" In this parable, Jesus is saying, why not give all of yourself? It has been said that we do not have to be much of a man or woman to come to Jesus. We just need to give Him all that we are.

The man who came to Jesus was a ruler; he had power and wealth. He was a good man and was interested in eternal life. Jesus went to the basic problem that hinders the search for eternal life with His question, "Why do you call Me good? None is good, save one that is God." The beginning of the search for eternal life is the realization that we are not good. Only God is good. Jesus is God. He claimed to be the same as the Father when He said, "He who has seen Me has seen the Father." In the book of Philippians, Paul wrote, "He (Jesus) thought it not robbery to be equal with God, but made Himself of no reputation and...took upon Himself the form of a man." Jesus was saying that if the man realized Jesus was good, that He was God, and that He was the promised Savior, and if he trusted in Him, he would have eternal life.

Jesus went right to the heart of this man's problem. He had done all the things of the law, but his wealth was his god. Jesus did not invite many to follow Him, but He did invite this man. The condition of following Jesus was to first get rid of his god, then of his wealth, with its associated power and prestige. The sad part of this story is that the man refused, even after Jesus showed him the way to end the search for eternal life. Jesus wanted all of him.

Many of us have our little gods that keep us from following after Jesus: our things, our leisure time, our preoccupation with success, and our bent to have our own way and do our own thing. It is not wrong to have these things under His control and leadership. Jesus simply must be first. He must be our God, and these other things then become tools we use to serve Him. His disciples noted that this saying was very hard, to which Jesus answered that it was impossible for man, but not for God. This means that we cannot put Jesus first without His help.

SEEING AND HEARING BUT NOT UNDERSTANDING

LUKE 18:31-34

Ask ten people who call themselves Christians what a Christian is, and you will probably get several different answers. Why is this? It could be that we really do not know what the Bible says about being a Christian, or that we don't understand it.

In this passage, Jesus told His closest followers what was going to happen to Him, but they did not understand. He stated it very plainly by prophesying that: 1. He was going up to Jerusalem, where all the things that the Old Testament says about Him would come true; 2. He would be delivered to the Gentiles. Gentiles are all nations that are not Jews - the Romans in this case. This is because the Jews did not have the authority to put anyone to death under Roman rule; 3. He would be mocked, abused, spit upon, beaten, and put to death; 4. He would rise from the dead the third day.

Why did they not understand what Jesus told them? It was because this was not their concept of the purpose and role of the Messiah. They believed the Messiah would be a ruling monarch who would sit on the throne of King David and put down the Romans. Only after His prophesies came to pass did His disciples truly understand, and it changed their lives. The Bible says that they turned the world upside down!

I think that we do not understand because of the same problem. We have our preconceived ideas about Jesus, God, heaven, hell, death, judgment, and many other spiritual things. We are ignorant of the Word, and our understanding is based on concepts which make provisions for the lifestyle we want to live. We make our religion fit what we want to do. This will not work.

The Bible tells it all: the way to live, the way to die, the way to salvation, the way to victory, and the way to deal with all the problems of life. We hear and see, but we already have our minds and hearts made up. Jesus said, "You shall know the truth and the truth shall make you free." He is the Truth and only as we submit to Him can we understand the Truth.

By Faith We See

Luke 18:35–43

If Jesus passed by and stopped to ask us, "What shall I do unto thee," what would we say? Most of us would even miss the question. He did not say, "What can I do for you," but rather, "what shall I do unto you?"

Most of us would have a list of things already in our mind that we would request of Jesus. But how many of us would ask Him to do something to us, something in us, some life-changing touch that would make us more like Him? How many of us would ask simply that He would open our spiritual eyes that we may see the wonder of His salvation?

The blind beggar was interested in only one thing—that he might see. He risked the ridicule of the crowd and possibly the rebuke of Jesus Himself, but it was worth it. Obviously, he had heard about Jesus. He had gotten reports from someone about the power and compassion of this man called Jesus. He also realized that Jesus was the promised One who was to come from the tribe of Judah, a descendant of David. He also realized that Jesus was his only hope. He cried aloud until Jesus came and stood at his feet. Jesus healed this man and commended him for his faith. The man asked the impossible, believing that Jesus was able to do for him that which He was doing for others.

We do not ask for sight because we do not realize we are blind. This man knew his condition and his need. We must also know that without Jesus we are hopelessly and helplessly blind spiritually. He is our only hope of salvation, and when we understand this, we will cry out, "Jesus, thou Son of David, that I may receive my sight."

Today, people have their trust in everything but Jesus. We tip our hat to Him, go to church once in awhile, and try to have some honorable goals in life, but most of us have our faith in something other than Jesus. We are spiritually blind. By faith in Him and His power to do something to us, we, too, can see.

SEEKING TO BE FOUND

LUKE 19:1–10

In the story of Peter and the wolf, three unlikely characters started out looking for the wolf. They thought they had found him, but actually he found them, for he immediately put them to flight with fear.

In this account, Zacchaeus, a most unlikely character, is looking for Jesus. He is a chief publican, who gathers taxes from his countrymen for the Romans who occupy his homeland. The practice of these men was to take that which the Romans demanded and keep any additional amount they took for themselves. No wonder Zacchaeus was rich; all tax collectors were.

Zacchaeus was a small man and could not see Jesus because of the crowd. He climbed up a tree just to get a look at this man he had heard so much about. He obviously had heard wonderful stories about this man who claimed to be the "Son of God." To his surprise, Jesus looked up the tree and spoke to him. He asked Zacchaeus to come down and take Him to his house.

Zacchaeus thought he was looking for Jesus, but Jesus knew the heart of this little man before He ever saw him. Jesus was looking for Zacchaeus. Like Peter and the wolf, Jesus had a much greater impact on Zacchaeus' life than he expected. As Jesus ate with him and shared his life with him, this little man was saved. As evidence of his salvation, he confessed and repented. To confess is to admit error; to repent means to turn and go the other way. He pledged one-half of his goods for the poor, and to those he had taken from, he would return four to one. That is repentance! But, oh, what he had received! Zacchaeus had received eternal life, a life of peace and assurance with the Savior.

There was some criticism from the "Holy Bunch," but Jesus said, "I have come to seek and save that which is lost." I used to say that I "found Jesus," but the more I read the Word, the more I realized that He found me. He was looking for me all the time. All I did was respond to His invitation once we met. And, like Zacchaeus, my life has not been the same since!

GOOD SERVANTS, BAD SERVANTS, AND REBELS

LUKE 19:11–27

Jesus was on his way to Jerusalem to endure the final chain of events linked to His trial, abuse, and crucifixion. Many were following because they thought He would become the mighty King, once He arrived at Jerusalem. Even His apostles did not fully understand that Jesus, as the promised Messiah, was to suffer and die. They did not want this kind of king. They did not realize what a great and mighty price must be paid for the sins of the world, but Jesus did. He knew the Old Testament Scriptures which say, "...and with His stripes we are healed and the Lord hath laid on Him the iniquity of us all." (Isaiah 53:5-6)

Jesus, in this parable, pointed out several things. First, He showed that He was going away, and that He would be back. Second, He showed that He would leave certain servants behind to look after things until He returned. These servants are His disciples and those of us who have trusted Him as Savior and Lord of our lives. We have been given certain abilities and opportunities to occupy and build on the good news of the free gift of eternal life He made available.

Some of us are good servants and some are bad servants. The faithful servants will be rewarded on His return and the unfaithful will be rebuked and chastised when He returns. We are not to just hang on to that which we have freely received. We are to be fruitful and multiply by helping others to find the way and by disciplining ourselves to accomplish His will in our own personal lives.

The rebels are those who reject His rule and His free gift of eternal life. They basically say, "Don't bug me, Jesus, I'll do it my way. I don't need anybody to rule over my life. I don't need you or your direction." Good servants, bad servants, and rebels will occupy the world until Jesus comes. The most important question is, which group are we aligned with?

THE KING IS COMING

LUKE 19:28–40

Jesus was very careful and deliberate in His instructions concerning the colt. This was the fulfillment of the Old Testament prophecy which said that the Messiah would come humbly, riding on a young donkey.

Remember that in the preceding scripture, Jesus had spoken a parable related to His return in power and glory to rule over the earth with His faithful servants. But now, in keeping with the time of His ministry on earth, He comes into Jerusalem as a humble servant riding on a donkey.

The people laid their coats and palm branches before Him as they proclaimed Him the King sent by the Lord. They had seen His mighty works and somehow hoped that He would become the King of Israel who would reign from Jerusalem. They wanted to bring His great power against Rome and all other enemies of the nation. Little did they know that He was riding to Jerusalem to be judged by the Jewish council and to be put to death on the cross by the Romans?

This is called the triumphant entry of Jesus into Jerusalem, and so it was. For without the beating, the humiliation, and the execution on the cross, we would have no hope. It was here that Jesus defeated the devil on our behalf, the great triumph for us by the Lord Jesus Christ, the King of Kings!

The Pharisees rebuked Jesus for the behavior of the crowd and demanded that He quiet them. Jesus said, "If they don't shout, the rocks will." This day was predetermined by God the Father in times past, and nothing could stop it, as long as Jesus was willing to suffer through the events at that time. The King was coming, and He is coming again. This time, He came as the humble servant; next time, as the righteous reigning judge!

DESTROYED FOR NOT KNOWING

LUKE 19:41–44

Ignorance of the law is no excuse in our system of justice, and so it is in God's system. There is something built into us that tells us we will be breaking the law if we run a red light. We did not have to attend a seminar on red, yellow and green traffic lights to be sure we know. We know because we are raised in an environment that teaches this truth.

The Bible teaches that none of us have an acceptable excuse not to know about God. Creation cries out that He is God and that those gods we make with our own minds or hands are products of our creation. The gods which we make and imagine cannot be greater than the One who created us. So we, too, are without excuse.

Jesus looked out over Jerusalem and became so broken over the condition of its people that he wept. He wept for two reasons. First, He knew that a time was coming for her destruction. Jesus said that not one stone would be left on the other; the destruction would be so complete. The death and destruction that was to come on Jerusalem was so bad that it brought the Lord to tears. These tears were more bitter because of the second reason. Jesus knew that the people of Jerusalem had rejected His coming as a revelation of the promised Messiah. Had they received Him as the Christ, the Son of God, this judgment would not be coming. With a broken heart, Jesus said, "Because thou knowest not the time of thy visitation."

What do we see as we look out over our city? Do we see friends, neighbors, relatives and associates headed for the coming "destruction?" Do we see them as being without excuse for not responding to the truth of Christ? Does it bring us to tears, send us to our knees in prayer, and drive us to share the truth with them? Look out over your nation, state, and city and ask God to let you see them through the eyes of Jesus.

WALK YOUR TALK

LUKE 19:45–48

It is so easy to find fault and criticize. It is so much easier to see the speck in our brother's eye than the chip of wood that is in our own eye. Jesus hated sin while He was here on earth, but had a divine love for the sinner. This truth was the driving force for His actions.

When Jesus went into the temple in Jerusalem, He was angered by the use of the temple to buy and sell animals for the sacrifices. The sellers were taking advantage of the poor people who had come a long distance to observe the religious days. They were charging too much and were too selective in the animals that were fit for sacrifice. The people were forced to buy an animal from the temple seller that would be suitable for sacrifice.

Jesus was angry at this practice and He forced them out of the temple. "My house is the house of prayer," he said, "and you have made it a den of thieves." After he forced them outside, He began teaching daily in the temple. His walk matched His talk. He demonstrated with His actions that the temple was a place of prayer, worship, and study of God's Word.

What would Jesus think if He visited our place of worship? Would He see a gathering of people who were preoccupied with doing business as usual rather than interested in prayer, worship, and Bible study? Would He say that our walk does not match our talk? There is a chorus which says, "Let us put away our cares and concentrate on Him and worship Him."

John warned the church at Laodicea when he wrote, "I would that you wert cold or hot. So then because thou art lukewarm, and neither cold nor hot, I will spew thee out of my mouth." (Rev. 3:15b-16) Was this another way of saying your walk does not line up with your talk? The only business we need to do at church is His business. He wants us to worship Him, see Him in the Word, communicate with Him in prayer and share Him with others.

QUESTIONS PRODUCED BY REJECTION

LUKE 20:1–8

After the triumphant entry into Jerusalem, Jesus began teaching and preaching in the temple while the chief priests and scribes "sought to destroy Him." (John 19:47) Even though He had demonstrated from the Word and by His deeds that He was the Son of God, they still rejected Him. Not only did they reject Him, but they sought opportunities to trap Him in His teachings and thereby establish a way to destroy Him. This group continually questioned Jesus, not for enlightenment but for entrapment, to show themselves right and Jesus wrong. These questions were motivated by jealousy, hate, and rejection of truth.

This is the tactic used by the devil in the garden of Eden. There he said to Eve, "Did the Lord say...?" Questions about that which is true and fundamental, for the purpose of rejection and destruction, will lead to self-destruction. The devil has his coming. The bumper sticker, "Question Authority," exemplifies this attitude in our day. It is good to question in the right way so that principles and beliefs may be confirmed in our hearts and minds, but to question simply because someone is in authority goes against God's plan. The Bible says that we are to submit to authority as unto God. The presence of authority in our lives is a test of our pride and humility, and often we flunk these tests.

Again, Jesus answered a question with a question. He knew their hearts and that they must deal with this question themselves if they were ever to be reconciled to God. The question was, "Who sent you, Jesus, and by what authority do you teach and preach this gospel?" The answer was in His question, "The baptism of John, was it from heaven, or of men?" John also came by the authority and anointing of God, but they rejected this, too!

Rejection of truth produces questions that hunt desperately for justification of the rejection. Jesus said "...I am the way, the truth and the life; no man cometh unto the Father but by Me." (John 14:6) He welcomes questions, but when He gives the answer, we must accept it and live by it.

NO MORE CHANCES

LUKE 20:9–18

Jesus had just dealt with the scribes and chief priests about His authority to do the things that He did. In this scripture Jesus seems to continue dealing with His authority and His true identity as the Son of God.

In this account, Jesus uses a parable that shows a landowner who planted a vineyard and turned it over to men who were trained and experienced in the raising and harvesting grapes. These men took over and rejected the authority of the owner, those sent by him and even rejected his son and killed him.

This seems to be a picture of God preparing a nation to show "His fruit" of love, grace, and judgment. This nation would be a "chosen generation" and a "peculiar people." The husbandmen were trained priests and scribes who were responsible for the spiritual maturity of this people. The servants are prophets sent to point out flaws in the spiritual conditions of the people and the error of the leadership. They were sent to plead on behalf of God to be fruitful and show God strong in their lives as individuals and as a nation. The prophets were rejected and abused by the high priest and scribes. Even God's Son was rejected and killed by this same group when He was sent by the Father as the ultimate revelation of God's will for their lives.

As a result, God opened up the opportunity for salvation and the spirit-filled life to all people. The vineyard became the world. Israel was no longer to be the only source of His revelation. Not only did Jesus stress that others would be made a part of the vineyard, but he also showed that the high priests and scribes would be needed no more. He became the High Priest for all believers and the indwelling Spirit becomes our Scribe as He helps us understand the Word. We too must recognize Jesus as the Son of God and receive Him as our personal Savior. God gives us opportunity time and time again to decide what we will do with Jesus. Nevertheless, there will come a time when this chance is gone forever.

YOU CAN'T OUTSMART GOD

LUKE 20:19–26

It is amazing that the chief priest and scribes perceived that the parable of the wicked husbandmen was about them, yet they proceeded to do exactly as the parable predicted. They sought to have Jesus killed by outsmarting Him. It is amazing that people today perceive that the Scriptures show them lost without Jesus, yet continue in their way.

The scribes tried to trap Jesus by seeking His answer to the question about giving tribute to Caesar. Their approach was amazing. They expected the promised King to take the throne of David and overthrow the Romans, yet their question was designed so that the answer could be used to accuse Jesus before the Romans. Jesus' answer was beautiful. First of all, He let them know that He saw right through them, once again verifying His authority, His power, His wisdom and His patience, even with this group of hypocrites. Then He illustrated a truth that is ageless. The coin bore Caesar's image, so give it to him; submit to him under the law of the land. Jesus also said, "Give to God that which is God's." In other words, Jesus was asking them whose image was stamped on them. God's image should be stamped on them, and they should submit their lives to Him.

So it is with us. The Internal Revenue Service Form 1040 bears the superscription of the federal government on it. We must render to the IRS that which is the government's. At the same time, we must commit our lives to Jesus to be fully directed by His control as the Word and the Holy Spirit direct. The demands of the Internal Revenue Service provide a way for us to submit to the authority of government. We must submit to them as an expression of our desire to submit our lives to Jesus. By so doing, we become a testimony to His power in our lives. Let us not be found trying to outsmart God!

THE LIVING GOD IS GOD OF THE LIVING

LUKE 20:27–38

Little children often ask if there will be pets in heaven. When their favorite dog or cat dies, they wonder if they will ever see it again. These are honest questions for little children but not for mature Christians. This kind of preoccupation with the things that are dear to us and satisfy our desires here on earth tends to bring heaven down to our level. When we do this, it is no longer God's heaven but our heaven. The same thing happens when we draw a mental picture of God. We know of His attributes, as described in Scripture and as exposed by Jesus here on earth, but this is only a passing glimpse of God. He is so much more, and so is the Heaven of His creation.

The Sadducees didn't believe in the resurrection, and since Jesus preached it, they set out to trap Him. The example they gave was earth-bound and limited to a fleshly mind. His ways are not our ways, and our minds cannot comprehend His order of things except as the Holy Spirit gives us understanding from His Word.

Again, Jesus was very patient with these Sadducees who continually rejected Him. This is a glimpse of heaven as it relates to the closest human relationship on earth, husband and wife. This earthly relationship was designed by God to be more like the coming relationship between Christ and the church than any other human relationship. Even so, Jesus pointed out that heaven is far above this.

Jesus gave a picture of heaven by showing clearly that our God is alive and is the God of the living. The Old Testament that these Sadducees loved to quote and live by says that Moses referred to the Lord at the burning bush as the Lord and God of Abraham, Israel, and Jacob. These great men of the faith died in the flesh many years before. Since God is the God of the living, these dead saints must still be alive, waiting the resurrection of the body to rejoin their living souls. The Sadducees quoted Moses and so did Jesus. You cannot outsmart God. He is the living God and the God of the living.

THE SON IS OLDER THAN THE FATHER

LUKE 20:39–47

Some of the scribes who heard Jesus' response to the question of the resurrection were impressed with His answer, because many of them believed in the resurrection. But mostly, they were scholars of the Word and loved to debate the Scriptures and hear others expound on them.

They decided that He was really a man of the Word, so they did not need to test Him along those lines anymore. They were satisfied with His knowledge of the Word. Now it was time for Jesus to show them that even in their great, scholarly approach to the Word, they were not very smart concerning the deeper meaning of the Scriptures. These scribes held to the proposition, clearly set out in the Old Testament, that the promised Christ would be a descendant of King David. They had, however, missed the greater point of the Scripture in that this descendant of David was also his Creator. Jesus, the Son of David, was older than David. The Bible says that Jesus was with the Father at the creation of the earth. Jesus used the inspired words of David himself to show this truth. If David called Him Lord, how is He then his son? Jesus is David's son, and Jesus is David's Lord. This can only be a result of the virgin birth. God the creator became an embryo in the womb of a virgin girl, Mary, a descendant of King David. Jesus is David's son through Mary, but His father is God, so He is David's Lord.

In their pride and pomp, the scribes displayed their knowledge of the Word, but Jesus used this simple truth of the Scriptures to show how little they really understood. We, like the scribes, cannot boast in our knowledge of the Word, for it is revealed in its true meaning by the Holy Spirit. Jesus warned the people not to be proud of their knowledge of the Word, but to humble themselves and submit to its admonitions. Practice the Word. That is the evidence of true understanding of its meaning. We should live like Jesus is the creator God, and not just a good, Jewish prophet who came as a descendent of David years ago.

GIVING IS RELATIVE

LUKE 21:1–4

Consider two people. One is in the fifty percent tax bracket. Poor fellow, at this point, every additional dollar he makes is taxed 50 cents. He has taken all the deductions, the depreciation, the contributions, the IRA's, the interest paid and so on. The other person is going to get back all the tax that was withheld from his paycheck. He is in the zero percent tax bracket. Which one of these men is the most financially secure?

The difference is that the first man made $250,000.00 last year and the other made $12,500.00. Now, who is the poor fellow? It is all relative to the number of dependents they have, the investments, indebtedness, and the many other factors used to determine the income tax. Strangely enough, the man that made the $250,000.00 may be on the verge of bankruptcy. He may be engulfed in debt and poorer than the man who made $12,500.00. It is all relative.

In this account of the widow's mite, Jesus points out that the rich gave and hardly missed it, while the widow gave all she had. The greater sacrifice of giving is relative to what each had to start with. In another parable, the rich, young ruler turned sadly away when Jesus suggested that he give all that he had to the poor. Wealth was his god. Zacchaeus gave half of all he had and promised to reimburse, four to one, all that he had taken falsely. He gave up his god and received the Savior as his new Lord. The poor widow gave all that she had because God was her provider and already Lord of her life. She was richer than them all.

There are other areas of giving that are also relative. How much of yourself have you given to God? Are there areas of your life that you refuse to turn over to the Savior? There are those who appear to be giving much of their time to His work. The question is, how much are we holding back? Are we investing our time teaching others, sharing Christ with the lost, with children, with friends and family? We must be like the widow and give all that we have to accomplish the task Jesus set before us.

BIG ANSWER TO A LITTLE QUESTION

LUKE 21:5–24

The question was: When would the great temple in Jerusalem be destroyed? In His answer, Jesus went beyond the point of the question and worked His way to the time of the destruction of the temple. He spoke of the times which would precede His return to earth and gave a warning and encouragement concerning things that would happen after the temple was destroyed.

There will be those who claim to be the Christ. This is deception, so pay no attention to them. There will be wars between nations, with great political turmoil, but this will not be the end. This is the political upheaval with the wars like World War I, World War II, Korea, Viet Nam, Arabs and Jews, and on and on. There will be no end to this until Jesus comes back to rule. There will be disasters in nature, such as earthquakes, famines and fearful sights. Mount St. Helens is an example, with its eruptions and accompanying earthquakes. It is equally upsetting to see the children and adults that are starving in many other parts of the world. All of these things are indicative of the upheaval of nature which must occur before the end.

Jesus also told of the persecution of those to whom He spoke. In the midst of these warnings, He promised to provide them with wisdom and words to speak. Jesus encouraged them with the assurance that their suffering would be used as a great testimony to Him. We see this in the persecution of the disciples: Peter crucified upside down, Stephen stoned, others killed by the sword, and Paul imprisoned, stoned, beaten and eventually executed. All these were living testimonies of the victory of Jesus in life, persecution, and death.

Then He comes to the destruction of the temple. When Jerusalem is surrounded by armies, its destruction will be brutal and complete. Young mothers and breast-feeding babies will perish. Many of the people of Israel will be killed, and others will be carried off to captivity. This all came to pass as Jesus predicted.

What a big answer to such a small question. The big question is what to do in times of distress. The answer is always Jesus.

AN ANSWER BEYOND THE QUESTION

LUKE 21:25–28

In this passage Jesus is not content with merely answering the disciples' question about the destruction of the temple. He goes far beyond in time to His second coming. Somehow there will be visible changes in the sun, moon, and stars in the heavens. In addition, there will be "roaring waves" in the sea, which indicates unusually high tides or perhaps tidal waves resulting from earthquakes as nature trembles at His coming.

On the political scene, nations will be under great stress, and the stress caused by these events will be so frightful that some will actually die of heart failure. Other places in the Scripture indicate that just before He returns a "great tribulation" will come on Earth that will last for seven years. It is said that a loaf of bread will sell for a day's wages as the world economy falls apart. During the depression of the 1930's, people committed suicide over financial loss. There will be much more personal stress as a result of these events.

Many other distressing things are described, but Jesus ends with a word of victory for those who belong to Him. To those who have trusted Him as Savior and Lord He said, "Lift up your heads." We are to lift up our heads and our hearts and look for him, for He will come again and redeem us from all this. In the book of John, Jesus said, "Let not your heart be troubled...I go to prepare a place for you...I will come again and receive you unto myself, that where I am, there you may be also..." (Jn. 14:13)

Jesus went beyond the disciples' question to assure them that no matter how difficult and stressful their situation becomes, they could always look to Him. As Christians, we have the same assurance. He will never allow a difficulty to overcome. He will always provide a way through our difficulty and will strengthen our faith in the process. Keep looking up when things get tough.

SPIRITUAL WEATHER WATCHING

LUKE 21:29–30

Being raised on the farm, it was always exciting to see the season's change. With every season change there was something vitally important that needed to be done. In the spring, there was a time to plant, but not too early or the cool nights would hinder the young sprout. The rains of late spring were important to the pasture as well as the cultivated crops. Then came the hot summer with harvest time following just before fall set in. It was important to kill the hog at the first winter frost. It was amazing how my dad could watch for the signs of the weather by the nature about him.

In this parable, Jesus points out that just as there are signs of the seasons by the behavior of nature, so there are signs of coming spiritual events. We are to read the Scriptures so that we will recognize the signs of His coming. He warns of the danger of being so caught up in the things of this world that we fail to recognize the signs of the spiritual times. He admonishes us to pray always as we watch for the signs of the times.

Jesus rebuked the Pharisees one time by telling them that they could look at the sunset and sunrise and predict the weather, yet they were blind to the signs that agreed with His claim to be the Son of God. The Bible teaches that if we know Him as Lord and Savior, we will escape the horrible times of the tribulation. Let us prepare and pray for that day when He will return to receive us unto Himself.

We must not get too caught up in analyzing the signs of His coming. It seems to me that if we are actively doing those things He told us to do, we won't have much time for this. Let us be busy about His mission so that we can touch as many lives as possible for Him before He comes.

Who Will Betray Him?

Luke 22:1–6

There are some who say that Judas betrayed Jesus because he believed that Jesus would show His great power when an attempt was made to arrest Him. These people reasoned that Judas thought his betrayal would accelerate Jesus' plan of action. This is not true, as this passage of Scripture clearly shows.

The time of the year was the Passover, and many people were coming to Jerusalem to celebrate this holy day, which commemorated the passing over of the death angel in Egypt. The desire of the chief priests and the scribes was to kill Jesus, but their fear of the people restrained them. The people accepted Jesus as a prophet with power to heal and to understand the Old Testament differently than the chief priests. The attention of the people was changing rapidly from the chief priests and scribes to Jesus as He taught and performed miracles among the people.

Then came the perfect opportunity, by the betrayal of Judas, to take Jesus with a minimum of exposure to the people. Judas agreed to identify Jesus at some place where there would be no people. Judas was aware of the places Jesus loved to go to pray or privately teach his closest disciples. It is obvious that Judas did not do this out of motivation to see Jesus show His great power. The Scripture says that satan entered into Judas. This can only happen when we let it happen. The Scripture says that Jesus is greater than satan, and the resurrection proves this. The Bible assures us that He who is within us is greater than he that is in the world. Note that Judas agreed to this act for money. If he was motivated to expose Jesus' power, why did he want money?

Judas betrayed Jesus because he allowed satan to influence him and because he let material things come before his devotion to Jesus. This is not an old story, it happens every day. We let the devil slip into our mind and motivate our actions. We let the affairs of this world take priority over our dedication and sensitivity to Him. We must be prepared lest we betray Him through pride, popularity, business, temper, or some other area of our life we have allowed satan to control.

Remember Who He Is And What He Did

Luke 22:7–23

When we think of characters of history, we remember who they were and what they did. We think of George Washington as the general of the Colonial Army and the first President of the United States of America—that's who he was. But just as important, we think of him kneeling in the snow to pray for his troops and for the infant nation; we think of his honesty as illustrated by the legend of the cutting of the cherry tree—that's what he did.

The Lord's Supper was established by Jesus as a remembrance of Him. "This do in remembrance of Me." In remembering Him, we must remember who He is and what He did. He is the Son of God, God Himself, the Creator of the universe. He is the epitome of love - that's who He is. He stepped down out of heaven from the position of equality with God the Father to become a man. He was born the same as you and me; He lived with pain, heartache and disappointment like you and me. He knew the laughter and the tears of growing up in a close family. Most importantly, He was tempted in ways beyond our imagination, without sin. He was physically abused and killed on the cross for our sin. He was separated from God the Father and tasted hell itself in full payment for our sins as He cried out, "My God, My God, why hast Thou forsaken me?" He arose from the grave on the third day to show His power and victory over death and hell and to show that this same victory is available to us by faith - that's what He did.

Jesus established the Lord's Supper and charged us to observe it in remembrance of Him. As we observe the Lord's Supper, let's always remember who He is and what He did. Let us also remember that He did these things for us personally.

The Measure Of Greatness

Luke 22:24–30

As little children we dream and fantasize about being some great pilot or law enforcement officer or movie star or space traveler. We dream of great accomplishments that will bring us the applause and praise of man. We also dream of, and experience to some degree, the deep, inner satisfaction of being the "greatest."

Jesus' disciples became caught up in the prospect of who would be greatest in His kingdom. In the example of the Gentile king, the characters were concerned with who would exercise power or be in the position of authority as the leader. Jesus very quickly pointed out that this was not the measure of great men in His kingdom. The leader in His kingdom would be the one who humbled himself the most, who was the most accomplished servant, and who was most like Him. The leader would give self, give rights and always focus on the main objective of love through the gospel. To sum it up, Jesus said that whoever was least among them would be greatest, just the opposite of what they thought. It is also just the opposite of the way the world thinks today.

We think as they did. We desire to be the chairman of the committee or the captain of the group, the one who gives all the orders and gets all the praise. Jesus' words to His disciples are applicable to us as we serve Him here and now. Jesus demands humility of us but we must choose the humble way.

Jesus is telling us to not worry about these things. This kingdom is His because His Father gave it to Him, and it is ours because He is giving it to us. Be great in it now by being a servant. There is a time coming when we will rule together with Jesus. For now, we are to seek first the kingdom of heaven and all these things will come. The way of Jesus is humility, and it can be ours by choice. That is the measure of greatness.

SATAN'S WORK, USED OF GOD

LUKE 22:31–38

The first two verses (31-32) show that satan desires to do us harm and magnify our weakness before God. We all have weakness in the flesh that brings dishonor to God. With some it is lying, with some it is bad language, and with others it is hurtful thoughts and actions. With all of us there is a measure of pride in doing it our way instead of His way.

These verses also show that we, like Peter, have someone who will help us against the evil one. The Bible says that He who is within us is greater than he who is in the world. It is interesting to note that Jesus prayed that Peter's faith would not fail, and this is what we all need. So many times when we fail under the attack of satan, we feel like an unworthy traitor toward the Lord. We must never lose faith, for the victory is in the Lord. If it were in us, we should rightly give up, but He has promised that He will never leave us or forsake us. Our victory is in Jesus.

The testing of satan, which is allowed by God, is a source of strengthening used by God in our lives. For example, we become arrogant when we are growing in the Lord and doing everything right. It is at this time that the devil comes to attack a weak point. God uses this to show that we have soft spots in our faith, and that He is not finished with us yet. James wrote that we should be glad when our faith is tried because this will work patience and perfection in our lives. (James 1:2-4)

Jesus foretold that Peter would deny Him three times before morning, but more important, He told Peter that he would be converted and be made stronger so that he, in turn, could strengthen the brothers. Take heart—Jesus never gives up on us. Don't give up on yourself. Even when satan comes after us, Jesus wants to turn it into a victory of spiritual strengthening.

HE TOO WAS TEMPTED

LUKE 22:39–46

There are times in our lives as Christians that we feel trapped and without hope. There are times when the pressures of life are so great that it seems impossible to continue. There are the pressures of business, the demands in just keeping the home together and functioning properly, and the pressures of school for the young people as more and more is required of them. This brings a heavy temptation to turn to self-pity, to feel singled out and picked upon, and to just give up.

Jesus went apart in the garden to pray, and He warned His disciples to pray that they not "enter into temptation." Jesus knew that the pressure was coming, and unless they prayed diligently they would enter into temptation, the first step toward sin and failure. If Jesus' disciples needed to pray when the times of pressure came, so do we.

Jesus then went a little farther into the garden to deal with an approaching temptation of His own. He knew that the hour was near. There would be beatings, humiliation, agony and, most of all, separation from God, His Father. He would endure hell for our sins. There, facing these horrible realities, Jesus sweat drops of blood and asked the Father to remove this cup, if it were possible. Then He offered up a prayer to the Father, which was the ultimate expression of faith and confidence: "Nevertheless not My will, but Thine be done." We must establish a relationship with Him that will bring us to this point, or we face defeat in the battle with temptation.

We have the example of the confidence of Jesus as He faced the greatest of all temptation. The Bible says that He was tempted in all points just like we are, "yet without sin." (Heb. 4: 15) It also says that there is no temptation that cannot be overcome, because He will help us resist it. (I Cor. 10: 13) He too was tempted.

Under Cover Of Darkness

Luke 22:47–53

Jesus had sweat drops of blood as He contemplated the price He must pay for our sins and as He talked to the Father, knowing that their intimate relationship would soon be broken. Jesus returned from praying to again find the disciples sleeping instead of praying. At that moment, Judas and the crowd who plotted Jesus' death came to Him in the garden. They came under the cover of darkness.

Several things happened in this encounter that show Jesus as the One in charge, rather than the chief priests and the crowd. It seemed strange earlier when Jesus asked if they had a sword, but now it makes sense. With one of the two swords, Peter cut off the ear of the servant of the high priest. This was not the real reason for the sword. The real reason for the sword was to give Jesus the opportunity to heal the ear and once again show the Jewish leaders that He was who He said He was. Once again He showed love, patience, and compassion for the religious leaders. Still, they rejected Him. He made true and practical His admonition that we love our enemies and do good to those who hate and despitefully use us.

When Jesus asked why they had not taken Him as He worshiped and taught in the temple, rather than wait for the cover of darkness, He was pointing out that they were acting according to the desire of the prince of darkness. Again He gave them another opportunity to repent and turn from darkness to the Light.

It is so much easier to betray Him in the darkness than in the light. It is so easy to pretend on Sunday at church and then under cover of the week's activities, to betray Him with our actions and words. Lord, help us to be faithful, even in the darkness.

THE LOVED IN SPITE OF...

LUKE 22:54–65

When Jesus asked Judas if he was going to betray the Son of Man with a kiss, Judas must have known that it was this of which Jesus had spoken at the Lord's Supper when He said that one would betray Him. Judas was given another chance as the love and grace of God was unfolded before his eyes and even touched him. But to no avail, for Judas carried out this plan devised by Satan himself. Jesus still loved Judas in spite of his betrayal.

Jesus predicted that Peter would deny Him three times before the rooster crowed the next morning. This, too, came to pass as Peter denied the accusation of being with Jesus and a part of His group. Jesus looked at Peter as the rooster crowed the third time, and Peter remembered Jesus' prediction and his own cocky rebuttal that this would never happen.

The difference in Peter and Judas is simple. Peter repented and Judas did not. Peter, the tough, burly fisherman who cut off the ear of the high priest's servant, burst into tears and fled after denying Jesus. He was broken and disheartened, but in his solitude he must have remembered that Jesus also said, "I have prayed for thee, that thy faith fail not; and when thou art converted, strengthen thy brethren." (22:31-32) Peter realized that Jesus loved him in spite of his weakness and human failure. Peter went on to be the strong, bold, humble, loving apostle of Jesus Christ.

We, too, deny our Lord in many ways as we reject His love, grace and salvation. Then one day, like Peter, we realize that He loves us in spite of our performances, and we too are converted. From time to time we fail as Christians, but the truth is, He still loves us in spite of, not because of our human abilities. Each of us has the potential to be another Simon Peter.

SEEING, SAYING, BUT REJECTING

LUKE 22:66–71

It was just a short time before that the crowd had ushered Jesus down from the Mount of Olives into Jerusalem, laying palm branches before Him. Now, the elders of the people, the chief priest, and the scribes, brought Him before the Jewish council for trial. Leadership can be, and often is, out of touch with the people and the truth. (Note our own Supreme Court and Congress as their rulings relate to busing, prayer in public schools, balancing the federal budget, abortion and so on. These actions are not aligned with the wishes of the majority of the people.)

More important is the spiritual aspect of this encounter. Again they asked Jesus if He was the Christ, the promised Messiah. He had answered this in many ways on many occasions in the past. He answered this from the Word, by the miracles He did, by the circumstance of His birth, and it was also answered by the testimony of others; but most still rejected the truth. Jesus responded to the question by reminding them that they would not believe Him if He answered. Then they asked Him if He was the Son of God, to which He replied, "Ye say that I am." Their response was, "What needs we any further witnesses?" They saw it, they said it, but they rejected the truth: Jesus is the Son of God.

It is the same today. People by the millions hear about Jesus, see Him in others and in His creation and even say His name. They somehow hope that He will leave them alone, let them live their lives as they choose, but at the same time not be too hard on them at judgment. They are seeing, saying, but rejecting. However, there is hope for those who receive Him... "as many as received Him, to them gave He the power to become the sons of God..." (John 1:12) Stop rejecting His will and His way for your life and receive Him now.

THE WORST DECISION IS INDECISION

LUKE 23:1-7

In the Army, we were taught as officers that we must evaluate any situation based on our training and then make the best decision in confidence. We were taught that indecision was fatal. To deliberate over the situation while the enemy advances on your position will eventually amount to a decision of indifference.

The multitude followed the leadership of the elders, the chief priests, and the scribes, and took Jesus to Pilate. They made a decision; it was wrong, but they decided to follow the advice of their leaders. Pilate heard the accusations against Jesus and questioned Him. His first conclusion, based on the facts at hand, was correct: "I find no fault in this man." This was his conclusion, but now comes the hard part, the decision. Pilate wavered under the pressure of the crowd and succumbed to indecision. Pilot reasoned that since Jesus was from Galilee, which was King Herod's area of responsibility, he would defer the case to him. Pilate made the right conclusion, but his action was not based on this conclusion but rather on indecision.

This indecision on Pilate's part would prove very costly. It gave him a detestable place in history. Pilot, knowing Jesus was a just man with no fault, allowed Jesus to be crucified, when it was within his power to release him. Pilot drew the correct conclusion, but failed to follow up with the right decision.

Indecision in everyday things can and will be very costly in our lives. To do nothing about Jesus is to end up alongside Pilate. To do nothing or continually study about a conclusion that God has given us will end in a defeated Christian life. Pray about it, look in God's Word, study the circumstances, seek His agreeing Spirit, and do it! When we follow this procedure, we can expect God to bless our decisions.

SEEING IS NOT BELIEVING

LUKE 23:8–12

Pilate found no fault with Jesus, failed to take a stand and sent Jesus to Herod, the Jewish king under Roman rule. Herod was delighted, because he had heard many things about Jesus. In fact, he had wanted to go see Jesus for a long time. Now, at last, Jesus was before him. Maybe Herod hoped to be entertained by the performance of a miracle. He bombarded Jesus with questions while the chief priests accused Jesus of claiming to be the Son of God, the Messiah, the King of the Jews. Herod and his military leaders made fun of Jesus and even put a beautiful robe on Him, like a king, and sent Him back to Pilate.

Herod heard about Jesus, and now he had seen Him, but he did not believe. Seeing is not believing. This unbelief brought him close to one who also rejected—Pilate. They had been enemies until this day, but their common rejection of Christ brought them close. The Bible teaches that people of like convictions will be found together. "Birds of a feather flock together."

We see this same sequence of events in a person's life today. In my own life I recall rejecting Jesus after hearing about Him. I remember indecision about what to do with Him, and this brought me closer to friends who felt the same way. Somehow, being friends with others who had also rejected Jesus justified my position. But then I saw Him through the revelation of the Spirit of God as a preacher told of Jesus' love for me. I had heard, and I had seen, but now I believe.

As Christians, we must go through a similar process. We are empowered with the ability to see spiritually as we are faced with many critical decisions. We must seek the answer through spiritual eyes and then believe in our decisions.

CONVICTION IS COSTLY

LUKE 23:13–25

When we are among those who believe as we do, it is easy to take a stand. The true test, however, comes when we are outnumbered by those who do not share our convictions or who are not willing to admit those convictions. Down with pornography! To that we say, "Amen," but who will march for an hour on Saturday around the stores that sell pornography? Who will walk along the sidewalk next to the street where our neighbors and associates can see us? Who will write a letter to the authorities and insist that our laws governing pornography be enforced? Convictions cost.

This scripture is one of the saddest accounts in the Bible. Pilate was so close to taking a stand that would have changed history's view of him and changed his life personally. He was convinced that Jesus was innocent of the charges brought against Him. Pilate's conviction in this matter caused him to try to persuade the people that Jesus should be released. He almost came to the point of pleading with them for their agreement to release Jesus, but they cried all the more for His crucifixion. Because of the crowd, Pilate did not act on his conviction and missed the greatest opportunity of his life.

Pilate's action is admirable until one considers that this man was in complete charge of the situation and had the power to pronounce the death penalty, send the accused to prison, or release him. Pilate had ultimate power over the situation. He was convinced of Jesus' innocence, yet he was willing to let the crowd sway him against his convictions. Failure to take action based on his conviction cost Pilate. It branded him forever as the one who sent Jesus to the cross.

Is your conviction costing anything? Are you ready to stand? To stand for our conviction can be costly from the world's point of view, but from God's vantage point, it will be rewarding.

TO MISS JESUS IS TO MISS IT ALL

LUKE 23:26–31

I heard about a man who had an uncanny way of making money. His life was dedicated to putting projects together to make money for himself and his friends. He was a member of a church but seldom attended. He was critical of the pastor and church leadership. His business dealings involved a group largely outside any spiritual activity. In his fifties, he became gravely ill and was not even aware of how much money he had. At the board meeting of a local bank he asked, "Do I have any money in this bank?"

He had it all, from the worldly point of view, money, property, expensive automobiles, but somehow he missed the impact of Jesus as He relates to everyday life. The man missed the personal relationship with Jesus, so he really missed it all.

In this scripture, Jesus is on the way to Golgatha to be crucified, with a great company of people following. The women were crying and lamenting after Him when He turned and told them that a greater tragedy was coming upon them. How could this be? Was it because a nation had missed Jesus and thereby missed it all?

The leadership of the church rejected Him, the national leaders rejected Him, and the intellectuals rejected Him. Jesus was living among them, teaching them and performing miracles among them. He was healing, comforting and teaching, while He lived such a perfect life that godless Pilate could find no fault in Him. You can have all this world offers, but if you miss Jesus, you missed it all.

We live in a day when the truth of Jesus is all about us. Churches, television, radio and personal friends constantly reveal the truth of Jesus Christ so that even a child can know and understand. Don't miss Jesus!

REAL FORGIVENESS

LUKE 23:32–38

Unconditional love is to love someone without the condition of performance. We try to apply this principle in our Christian walk. There is a companion principle shown in this scripture which is unconditional forgiveness. Jesus said, as He hung on the cross, "Father, forgive them, for they know not what they do." In spite of all they had done to Him and the agony of the moment, Jesus could still forgive.

We have a mindset which says that unless they repent or confess, then we cannot forgive. It is true that we should confess and repent of sins in our life. Day by day, moment by moment, circumstance by circumstance, we must confess to God and repent in order to live in His victory. But the truth of the matter is that we are forgiven even before we ask. We should practice this same type of forgiveness towards others.

When Jesus died on the cross, He took all our sin, past, present, and future, on Himself. The Bible says that the iniquity of us all was laid upon Him and with His stripes we are healed. We are forgiven in advance, but we must receive this by an act of our will. We receive it by confessing and repenting. We do not manufacture forgiveness by our good works of confessing and repenting, but rather we appropriate forgiveness that was freely given long ago when Jesus spoke to the Father about us saying, "Father, forgive them; for they know not what they do." He even helps us appropriate it by faith.

We need to practice this principle. We need to learn how to forgive those who wrong us and wait patiently for them to appropriate that forgiveness. Real forgiveness is forgiving someone even when the world says that they do not deserve it.

GRACE ON THE CROSS

LUKE 23:39–43

Grace has been defined as the cute little girl that sat on the front row in the second grade. It is also defined as carrying one's self with posture and proper confidence. But the grace of God is best defined as a gift we do not deserve and one so valuable we can never earn it. The ultimate expression of God's grace is Jesus on the cross, providing us with free access to the Father by His payment for our sins.

Eternal life is a free gift, bought and paid for in full by our Lord as He went through the agony of the cross. Our only part in this transaction is response. We certainly can do no more to earn our salvation than that Jesus has already done. Our response must be humility, confession, recognition, and receiving Jesus as our personal Lord and Savior.

This transaction is seen beautifully in the account of the thief on the cross. First, we see his humility as he rebuked the other thief for demanding that Jesus save them all from this execution. As he points out that he is a sinner and deserves what he is getting, we see confession. As he recognizes that Jesus has done nothing wrong, we see his humble recognition of Jesus as the perfect God-man. Then he makes a commitment of acceptance as he asks Jesus to remember him in His kingdom. This is a great expression of faith. As he hangs on a cross without hope of escape, the convicted man turns to Jesus, who appears to be in the same condition, and asks to be remembered after death.

Then comes the beautiful, simple expression of God's grace on the cross as Jesus said, "...today shalt thou be with me in paradise." Jesus is the same today and is longing for those who will accept His wonderful gift of eternal life.

THE DISAPPOINTMENT OF HAVING YOUR WAY

LUKE 23:44–49

Have you ever been so interested in a project that as time passed the project became foremost in your mind and heart? It almost became an obsession until it was at last finished just the way you wanted. Following the completion of such a project there sometimes comes an inner depression, a feeling of letdown. There is a realization that the project which seemed so right and important did not turn out as was envisioned. Chuck Colson shared how he spent an entire year, while he was counsel for President Nixon, pushing and lobbying a bill through Congress; only to find that some years later it really did not make the impact he thought it would.

In this scripture we see the dream of the scribes and Pharisees and high priest come true. This Jesus, who had caused them so much trouble, was finally put to death. But something unexpected happened in this process. The whole earth darkened as if God were hiding His face from the scene, and the veil in the temple tore in two. This was the veil that horses could not rip apart, yet it was ripped supernaturally from top to bottom. This veil separated the ark of the covenant, where the presence of God came down, from the people. The ark could be approached by the high priest only and by him only once a year. A Roman officer, standing near, praised God, even though he did not understand everything he was seeing. He heard Jesus' last words spoken to His heavenly Father and realized that Jesus was much more than a politician. What a disappointment for the people who came to witness that for which they had cried out, "Crucify Him! Crucify Him!"

But this was also a great victory, just as God had planned. The revelation of hope for you and me came to light as Jesus paid it all on the cross. Even those who had Him put to death saw this new hope, because He died for the sins of everyone. The tragedy is that many, then and now, did not appropriate the wonderful gift paid for by Jesus. The Roman officer did and so did many of his friends who looked on from afar.

STANDING ALONE FOR JESUS

LUKE 23:50–56

About the most unpopular and dangerous thing to do at this time in Jerusalem was to take a stand for Jesus. The disciples were gone and scattered, the women "stood afar off," or "followed after," but one man, Joseph of Arimathea, took a bold stand. He had already taken a risk since he was a counselor and had voted against the action of the council. I strongly suspect that this man had the respect of many people in high places. He had stood alone against the execution and humiliation of Jesus and survived.

Now he had the fortitude and conviction to go to Pilate and openly plead for the body of Jesus in order to see Him properly buried. Not only did he survive this action which identified him with Jesus, but he got his request. The account, in John 19, also identifies another who took a lonely, dangerous stand for Jesus at this time—Nicodemus. These two men took the body of Jesus and prepared it for burial, just as the Scriptures predicted and prophesied. These two men stood alone for Jesus at a time when it seemed that the whole world had rejected Him.

Standing alone is not easy and is not without cost. These men may have been set apart from that day forward, although you read little or nothing of them after this in the Scriptures. These men are recorded in history alongside Pilate, Judas and Herod, but history records that they stood alone for Jesus. Surely they made a difference for Christ while they were on the earth. More importantly, they probably have a special place in Heaven, even in His presence. Stand for Jesus! It costs, but it also pays. The reward that comes from standing for Him always outweighs the cost.

THE LIVING AMONG THE DEAD

LUKE 24:1–12

This passage of Scripture is so powerful and necessary to the Christian faith that almost every verse is loaded with truth linked to our salvation and worship practices. First, we see that Jesus arose from the grave on the first day of the week—Sunday. What better reason to worship the risen Lord on Sunday? Next, we see that the huge stone, too large for a woman, or even one man, to roll away, was removed from the opening of the grave site. This was done by the hand of God (possibly through angels) just as the veil in the temple was torn when Jesus died.

So, we have a new day of worship, Sunday, and a new way of worship, each believer having access to the mercy seat. A new day and a new way with liberty inscribed on both by the grace of God through Christ. All through this passage we see the affirmation of Christ as Savior and God. We see it by the presence and words of the angels, by the reaction of the women, and by the actions of the disciples and Peter.

The words of the angels to the women, "Why seek ye the living among the dead?" is a loaded question. First and foremost, these words ring out the truth that Jesus is not dead. He is alive. He is risen, just like He said. These words also say that those of us who have trusted Him as Savior and Lord of our lives are also "living." We live forever because of Him, but we are here among the spiritually dead. Our home and the kingdom to which we belong is in heaven, but we reside here on earth among these dead. Let us be busy awakening the dead about us so that they too may live.

Let us be careful that we do not become so caught up in the things of this world and the lifestyles of this earth that we are truly living like the dead. Jesus said that He wanted us to be in the world but not of the world. Be not unequally yoked to the dead or the dead things of this world. Be a breath of life and a ray of hope around the dead.

CLOSE ENCOUNTER

LUKE 24:13–35

There are many people who know all about Jesus but do not know him personally. I have known people who have gone to church and Sunday school for years and yet have not had a close encounter with Jesus. There are those who have memorized Scripture, but somehow have not received it into their heart in a way that will allow the Holy Spirit to introduce them to Jesus in a personal way.

It is like reading about a person until you know all about them, but never getting to meet that person and fellowship with him. I can know all the things about my wife, all the childhood stories and events that shaped her life, but I cannot know her intimately until we commit our lives to one another in a close encounter.

These good and faithful men on the road to Emmaus were followers of Jesus. They recognized Him as a "great prophet...mighty in deed and word..." They even had the latest information about Him, knowing that the women had gone to the tomb and found His body gone. They knew some believed that Jesus had risen and was alive. But somehow, all these things they knew about Him did not substitute for knowing him.

Then came the close encounter with Jesus as He walked alongside and listened patiently as they reviewed the recent events. He opened the Scriptures to them all the way back to the writings of Moses and showed them how it was written that these events would happen to the Messiah. He opened their hearts and eyes, and they knew Him! All the things they knew about Him could not compare to this close encounter with Him.

We need to know Him more and more each day. We need to fellowship with Him in each event of every day. He is there all the time. The tragedy is that He walks alongside us many times when we, like the men on the road to Emmaus, do not recognize Him and thus miss the opportunity to know the joy of a close encounter with Him.

ALL THINGS FULFILLED IN HIM

LUKE 24:36–48

Jesus never missed an opportunity to teach and impart truth while He walked with His disciples. I think He even created situations, or at least utilized circumstances known only to Him, that proved to be great learning experiences for His followers.

Many of these teachings were not understood until after the crucifixion and the resurrection. As the discussion and debate of His disciples concerning His resurrection became more intense, He suddenly appeared in their midst. The reaction was terror, which confirms that they did not fully understand His teaching.

Now, Jesus, in His patient and loving way, shows all present that it is really Him and that He has indeed risen from the dead. There was belief but no joy, there was understanding but still the fear, so Jesus opened the Scripture to them once again to show that the Old Testament prophesy concerning Him had been fulfilled. All things had now been fulfilled, so that repentance and remission of sins could be preached. Jesus then charged that they must be the witnesses of these things. They had seen, understood and received; now it was up to them to tell others.

Why did God save us? If it were only so that we could go to heaven, why not "save us and take us" in the same moment? We were saved for more than that. We are to be His witnesses and use every opportunity to share the Gospel with others. We are to be careful regarding our personal lifestyle so that we can say, "Touch me, look at me, and examine my life." Our lives must be a testimony that Jesus lives in us. Then it will be effective when we tell others how all has been fulfilled to allow them eternal life through Jesus Christ. We have seen, understood and received the free gift of eternal life. Now it is up to us to tell others.

PROMISED POWER PROVIDED

LUKE 24:49–53

Have you ever wondered how we can possibly do all that God told us to do? How can we ever believe unto salvation and receive all that Jesus has done for us as a free gift available only by faith? How can we have this kind of faith? Where does it come from? Then after we are saved, how are we to live the sanctified life that God demands? How can we establish a lifestyle that moves steadily toward perfection by the standard of God's Word? There is also the problem of understanding God's Word as He wants it to apply to a particular problem of the moment. Where are we to get the sensitivity to know when someone is lost or backslidden or hurting, and where do we get the ability to minister to these needs?

Jesus demonstrated the answer. He came down from heaven and allowed Himself to be as a baby. He lived in the most difficult time for his nation, Israel. He experienced life as we know it but was without sin. He suffered the ridicule and physical abuse of those about Him. He tasted hell for you and me as He died on the cross. He showed His power by coming back from the dead. He patiently explained and demonstrated the purpose for these events that we might believe and be saved by His wonderful grace.

Then He went a step further. He promised to send the Holy Spirit to live in each of us as a guide and inner power to do all those things that are humanly impossible. This He verified by ascending into heaven before a host of witnesses. Promised power to accomplish all the things He told us to do was provided by our Lord and King! To Him be power and riches and wisdom and strength and honor and glory and blessing forever and ever! Amen.

CONCLUSION AND CALL TO ACTION

I hope you were enriched in reading "A Little Light from Luke" half as much as I was in writing it. Maybe you are a private person, as I am, but I felt compelled to "pass on" the beautiful intimate relationship with my creator God.

Now I hope you will share it and pass it on to others. Start as I did with your family, then friends, associates and neighbors. Be bold in sharing your faith throughout each day with contacts like waiters, service people and others who help keep things working, receptionists, nurses, doctors and all others. Treat them as divine appointments and be a encourager for the Lord Jesus. If this is confusing and foreign to you, please begin with yourself. You can pray a simple prayer from a true heart and start a new life now. Admit to God that you have been living a life as you pleased without seeing His will and direction. Ask Him to forgive you and ask Him to rescue you by the grace extended through Jesus Christ on the Cross. Tell Him you want to receive Jesus as Savior and Lord (Boss!) of your life. Ask Him to direct your life His way from now on. Be sure to thank Him for the greatest gift known to man. Contact a minster of a church that preaches and teaches the true Bible. Tell them that you have decided to follow Jesus. Pray and ask God to direct you to the church of His choice.

Keep in mind that it is your privilege and responsibility to read the Scriptures and pray every day. Intimate relationships require meaningful communication. You talk to God by prayer, and you listen to him by the Scriptures. Make this a part of your daily life, and get ready for an exciting life with challenges that will strengthen you in the faith and bring you closer to Jesus.

A Little Light From Luke